Praise for Pamela Nickel Williams

"L. Ron Hubbard and his Church of Scientology touched thousands of people's lives, promising a better existence and a better world through its practices. Pam's harrowing and intriguing account of her childhood growing up under the influence of Scientology, with a horribly abusive father and a disengaged mother that Scientology not only couldn't help but ultimately caused even more damage to, shows the reality of what Scientology really does. It takes advantage of people, hurts them, and exacerbates their pain. Pam's writing gives you a series of snapshots of what it's like from a child's perspective to be forced to constantly be pushed and pulled about, seemingly at random by adults who have no idea what they are doing yet are so sure they are saving the world. Rarely have I seen anyone tell their story in such a raw yet effective way. This one is definitely worth your time."

– Chris Shelton: Msc, Author and Host of *Speaking of Cults*, a podcast about cults, coercive control, and recovery

———————————

"I just finished reading **Clearly Lies Are True.** It was a powerful, eye-opening experience. Pamela's book offers a raw, firsthand account of growing up in Scientology during the '60s and '70s—when L. Ron Hubbard was still alive and the religion was being practiced in rundown homes, surrounded by the free-spirited culture of the time. What struck me most was how the same patterns of neglect and manipulation I've personally witnessed were already present back then. The emotional weight of the story is heavy, especially around the unspoken sexual abuse the author, Pamela, endured at the hands of her father. It's heartbreaking that she carried that pain in silence for so long.

This book is ultimately a powerful testimony about the mistreatment of children within Scientology. Definitely worth reading if you're interested in the early days of the church and the lasting impact it had on its youngest members."
– **Katherine Spallino: Author of *The Bad Cadet:***
Growing Up in the Church of Scientology's Sea Organization

"*Pamela shares her experiences with clarity, wisdom, and emotional depth, turning her painful childhood into a source of profound insight. She invites people in to see the resilience and humanity that can emerge from dark places, and her strength is a beacon of hope for anyone seeking healing.*"
– **Rachel Bernstein: LMFT, MSEd,**
Host of IndoctriNATION,
**a weekly podcast about cults, manipulators,
and protecting yourself from systems of control**

"*Pamela's story is truly a gripping and powerful memoir of her upbringing in Scientology. Her detailed account takes readers on a journey, through her eyes as a child on the Royal Scotman, to becoming a teenage auditor, and even crossing paths with L. Ron Hubbard. Williams' narrative exposes the intricate web of truths and lies of the Scientology world and modern American life in the 1960s and 1970s. Pam's unflinching honesty and masterful storytelling make this book a must-read!*"
—**Caris Adams, Ed.D., University Instructor and Educator**

CLEARLY LIES ARE TRUE

A MEMOIR

CLEARLY LIES ARE TRUE

A MEMOIR

PAMELA NICKEL WILLIAMS

PAMELA NICKEL WILLIAMS PUBLISHING

CLEARLY LIES ARE TRUE

For information, permissions, and appearances, please contact:
Pamela Nickel Williams
clearlyliesaretrue2024@gmail.com

Book cover and interior design by Mermaid Cafe.

The text of this book was set in Adobe Garamond.

ISBN: 9798218670757
Library of Congress Control Number: 2025909325

Pamela Nickel Williams Publishing
clearlyliesaretrue2024@gmail.com

Printed in the USA.

DEDICATION

To my granddaughters,

Adeline and Evelyn

Know that you are loved beyond measure

May you live bravely and always speak your truth

Grammy

CONTENTS

INTRODUCTION

"It takes truth to live with a swiftly changing world.
Nothing less than truth can survive.
You cannot survive with anything less than truth."

– L. Ron Hubbard

The Ability Congress – Washington, D.C., 1957

I have often and seriously wondered which came first, my family's insanity or Scientology? Growing up as the daughter of early Scientologists, I sensed how secretive and different my family was from other families that I knew and observed. But as a child, I didn't understand how my parents' behavior, including their inability to nurture and care for me, emanated from their Scientology beliefs.

How were my parents' propensities toward certain thoughts, beliefs, and actions exacerbated and fueled by their personal experiences in Scientology? Were my parents genetically wired and

I

predestined to suffer from mental health issues and abusive tendencies, or was Scientology the catalyst that activated these pathologies?

Trying to answer these questions, or at least learn how my parents' beliefs evolved and influenced their actions, has guided my writing and my search for truth, in as much as it can be found. Yet the quest for truth can be an elusive pursuit. Most cults, like Scientology, prey on those who seek promises of healing physical and emotional brokenness. Dogmatic yet convincing beliefs and the enticement of spiritual elevation permeate cult mentality, leading many *"truth seekers,"* like my parents, down a perceived path of enlightenment.

My father, Paul, began his indoctrination, and subsequent journey into Scientology, after purchasing the book *Dianetics: The Modern Science of Mental Health*, published by L. Ron Hubbard in 1950. As a teenager, my father had been an avid science fiction fan, reading many of Hubbard's stories in his favorite magazine, *Astounding Science Fiction*. Eagerly devouring *Dianetics*, my father read it in one sitting from cover to cover, digesting and believing every word. The book *"spoke to him"* in a way that nothing else had. He was hooked!

Living in Wichita, Kansas, my father immediately began participating in *Dianetics* processing, and he attended many of L. Ron Hubbard's lectures in the very early days of Scientology at the Wichita Dianetics Foundation. Enamored by Hubbard, he quickly became one of a handful of loyal, faithful believers, and a devoted and dedicated follower. But, just a year after its opening, the Wichita Dianetics Foundation suffered financial issues and mismanagement, leading to its abrupt closure. Subsequently, L. Ron Hubbard packed up, left Wichita, and quickly opened the Founding Church of Scientology in Washington, D.C.

In 1957, shortly after my parents were married, they made the choice to follow L. Ron Hubbard, at my father's insistence, from the Midwest to the East Coast. For the next three years, my mother, Gloria, worked at the Founding Church of Scientology. During this time, my parents both became active members and leaders in the formation of the HAS—Hubbard Association of Scientologists, working closely with L. Ron Hubbard, and his wife, Mary Sue.

With its small but devoted following, Scientology was growing. Franchises were developing in other cities and membership was expanding, along with L. Ron Hubbard's bank account. However, tax evasion charges and fraudulent claims were all real, constant, and looming threats against his burgeoning empire.

One such claim occurred while my parents were in Washington, D.C. On April 5, 1958, FDA—Food & Drug Administration— inspectors visited the Founding Church of Scientology offices and seized 21,000 Dianazene tablets, basically a vitamin pill, which Hubbard had falsely claimed would cure radiation sickness. My mother witnessed the raid, and spoke of it often. As a practicing Scientologist, she sincerely believed it was unjustified. Through her narrow, colored lens, it was tantamount to an attack on her personal beliefs, as well as those of Scientology and L. Ron Hubbard.

But in 1959, the year after I was born, Hubbard left claims such as these far behind him and headed to England, to live at Saint Hill Manor, a large mansion nestled in the idyllic English countryside, that he had purchased with his profits from Scientology.

As he planned his departure, Hubbard persuaded some

Scientologists, who had been part of the HAS in Washington, D.C., to follow him to England. Many other Scientologists, like my parents, who had been a part of Scientology since its inception, were torn by the prospect of moving, especially across the Atlantic Ocean.

This is where my story begins. Through personal accounts of my childhood, and teenage years, multiple narratives emerge and intertwine. These include sexual abuse, at the hands of my father, my parents' mental and physical health issues, and firsthand accounts of how the adults, who were charged with my well-being, were out of control. As my family unraveled, I learned to adapt and become resilient, ultimately choosing my own identity and path to freedom as a survivor of both sexual abuse and cult mentality.

My timeline of events and lived experiences are true, to the best of my knowledge, as well as referenced Scientology history and factual records that I have included. In sharing my journey, it is my hope that those who struggle as I have with familial dysfunction, sexual abuse, and controlling beliefs will find resolution, as well as forgiveness. Wishing you strength and courage in your own personal search to heal, as you accept and discover a path to truth that leads you to the freedom you deserve.

❦

PART 1

THE BEGINNING,
CIRCA 1961

Building memories meant to last a lifetime, we posed next to a sign that read, **Continental Divide – Loveland Pass – Elevation 11,988 feet.** A location where the North American continent literally divides itself.

Huddled between my mother and father, I sat barefoot on the cement slab that covered the rocks below us. Wearing just shorts and a t-shirt, the sun warmed my small uncovered arms and legs. The wind blew loose strands of my blonde hair across my cheeks and nose, and into my face.

My mother's long legs, crossed at the ankles, stretched out from inside her white shorts. Her thin sandaled feet touched the ground below us. A sleeveless lightweight cotton blouse covered her tall frame and fluttered in the breeze against her torso. Shielded by her black-framed sunglasses, her eyes were hidden. As her lips parted, a smile radiated across her face, revealing a small dimple in her left cheek.

Leaning against my father, his right arm enveloped me, while the dark black hair on his forearm rested against my bare shoulder. His large hand firmly held my tiny wrist still as it lay upon my uncovered knee. In his other hand, he casually held a lit cigarette between his index and middle fingers. Dressed in a short-sleeved plaid shirt with buttons undone at the top, his white undershirt exposed his thick neck.

Gazing intently at the photographer, our matching green eyes squinted in the sunlight as a kind tourist took our picture at what seemed like the top of the world.

A moment in time, captured in a black-and-white snapshot as we traveled by car across the United States in the summer of 1961. I was almost three years old. My little brother had not yet arrived. Just me, my parents, and Scientology. A perfectly lopsided triangle.

TIME TO MOVE,
DENVER, COLORADO

Driving to the construction site, we passed mountains, lots of them. I sat in the back seat of our pale blue 1959 DeSoto Chevrolet, staring out the window. With no seatbelt to constrain me, I got up on my knees so I could see the white lines on the black highway as we drove down the curvy road.

Daddy held his lit cigarette in one hand, while his other hand rested on the steering wheel. Mommy and daddy talked mostly in quiet voices as we drove. Watching the mountains pass by, I wondered what our new house would look like. Mommy had told me that we'd live closer to my cousins, who I'd never met. I was curious. What would they look like? Would they be nice?

Lost in my daydream, I felt the car stop suddenly. I looked at mommy and daddy in the front seat. They'd turned toward each other. Daddy's voice was louder now. "Well, Gloria, I hope you're happy, now that we're out of D.C. It's what you wanted, right? You couldn't wait to leave."

Mommy turned her head and looked out the front windshield at the empty road. There were no cars in front of us or behind us. I watched her as she took a deep breath, then blew out the air, like she was blowing up a balloon.

"Paul, I thought we came to an agreement. We both acknowledged that we wanted to move."

"Agreements and acknowledgments! Don't make this sound like an auditing session, Gloria. We both know who made the decision. It was you! Not me! I didn't acknowledge anything, except that you wouldn't follow Ron and Mary Sue to England."

"Paul," mommy answered, "Mary Sue knows about the baby. We're raising a family. That's important to her too. You know I talked to Jesse. He likes Denver, and so do his boys. And, we're lucky we got the G.I. loan to buy the house."

Mommy stopped and looked out at the road. Then she turned back toward daddy. "And, John and Millie are starting their own franchise here. We agreed to follow them."

I wasn't quite sure who John and Millie were, but I knew that Jesse was my uncle. Even though I'd never met him, mommy had told me about him. He was her older brother.

As mommy talked, I watched daddy's face. He didn't look happy. The more she talked, the redder his neck and face became. I studied the skin that stuck out from his white undershirt as it turned pink and then red. The color traveled up his neck, first to his cheeks, and then to the whole side of his face. He stared at mommy, but didn't say anything. I leaned forward a little to look at his neck, but quickly jumped back on the bench seat as daddy slammed his fist down onto the steering wheel. Then he started shouting at mommy. "That's right, Gloria! They left and we didn't follow them! Don't you remember Ron's words at the Congress in D.C., when he handed me my Clear Bracelet?"

Again, daddy slammed his fist back down onto the steering wheel, and shouted, "In case you didn't hear it, Ron told us we need to Clear this goddamn planet!" Then he pointed at his Clear Bracelet, and demanded, "So, Gloria, where the hell is your Clear Bracelet?"

Mommy just stared at him as he continued to shout and preach at her, "As Scientologists, it's our job, our purpose, to create more Clears. And what's the definition of a Clear?" Daddy crossed his arms over his chest and looked at mommy with mean eyes.

"It's someone who has..." mommy tried to tell him.

But daddy just yelled at her, "C'mon, Gloria! I'll tell you the definition. A Clear is a person at willing and knowing cause over his own life, his body, and his surroundings without a reactive or subconscious mind. Got it?!"

Abruptly, daddy opened the car door and got out. Standing next to the car, he threw his half-smoked cigarette onto the black pavement. I watched him from the back seat as he lifted his foot and stomped on it, leaving it twisted and broken on the ground.

Mommy sat in the front seat, looking very sad. I don't think she liked when daddy yelled at her. Maybe, I thought, mommy shouldn't say things that make daddy so mad. He wouldn't yell at her if she just said nice things.

We sat quietly, waiting for daddy to get back in the car. From the back seat, I could still see him. He walked down the road and stared out at the mountains around us. It seemed like he stood there a long time while mommy and I waited in the car.

Then I heard mommy sniffle. I could see the back of her head as it dropped forward. I watched as her shoulders gently shook. It sounded like she was crying. I didn't know what to do, so I looked out the window and watched daddy, to see if he was coming back to the car yet. Although mommy sat close enough to touch, I didn't reach out for her. I didn't know if I should.

Once she stopped crying, she turned around and looked at me in the back seat. Her cheeks were wet and her eyes looked pink. I tried to make her happy by smiling, but she didn't smile back. It was hard to make mommy happy.

When I looked out the window again, I saw daddy walking back. His face wasn't bright red any more, but he still looked kind of mad. He opened the car door, sat down in the driver's seat, and slammed the door shut. Reaching down, he turned the key and started the car. I watched as his silver Clear Bracelet slid and turned, hiding the raised "S" covered by two triangles, the symbol for Scientology.

As we started moving again, I wiggled around in the back seat. Tired of looking at the mountains, and not sure what would happen next, I laid down on the cool white vinyl, seat, and closed my eyes. In hushed voices, I heard mommy and daddy talking again. As I listened, bits and pieces of their conversation traveled from their mouths in the front seats, to my ears, where I lay quiet and still.

I heard mommy tell daddy something else about John and Millie. Daddy answered her with words I didn't understand, except for the word Scientology, which I'd heard often, but didn't like. Whenever mommy and daddy talked about it, they always seemed mad. With my eyes closed, the movement of the car made me feel like I was being rocked back and forth. But just before I fell asleep, I heard mommy tell daddy, "After the baby."

• • •

Standing in the wood-framed doorway of our new house, I held mommy's hand, in the summer before the snow, before the belly, before the sadness. As we walked through each of the framed spaces, not yet defined by walls, she pointed to where the kitchen cabinets and appliances would be placed. I followed her through each empty part of the house, skipping and jumping with joy. My sandaled feet landed on the plywood floorboards, echoing our arrival throughout the open walls.

While mommy stayed in the kitchen area, I danced down the open hallway, peering into each partially constructed room, wondering which one would be mine. I was not quite four years old, but I could sense that mommy was planning out every detail of our new home as she stared through the wooden beams that sectioned off each area. Standing on the sawdust floor, strewn with bent nails, her feet protected only by her white rubber flip-flops, she paced the perimeter.

I stood close by and watched her as she studied each unfinished section of the room. A determined smile would suddenly appear on her face, soon to be replaced by a brief scowl. The skin between her eyebrows furrowed, creating three small lines that made her look like she might be thinking. Not wanting to interrupt her, I walked toward the back of the house and looked through the open framing at the backyard. It was just a dirt pile. No grass had been planted yet. I looked up and saw a large mountain looming in the distance. It looked huge! I wondered if it was the same mountain we'd driven past on our way to the construction site.

Suddenly, I heard mommy call my name, "Pammy, where are you?"

I'm right here," I yelled back. Feeling playful, I added, "Come and find me!"

I could hear mommy's flip-flops shuffle down the hall, across the sawdust and plywood boards. I giggled as her footsteps came closer and closer to where I was trying to hide. With no walls to duck behind, I decided to crouch down in a corner, holding my bare knees with my hands. I closed my eyes and waited.

"There you are!" I heard her exclaim.

I jumped up and ran to her, "You found me!" I shouted with glee as she reached for my hand and led me back down the hallway to the front of the house.

As she held my small hand in hers, I wanted to believe that mommy was happy. But after walking just a few steps, she dropped my hand and looked out the framed opening where the front door would be placed. I watched as her smile faded and her brow furrowed again. It seemed hard for mommy to stay happy for very long.

. . .

That winter, after we'd moved in, we awoke one morning to a blanket of white snow. It covered the walkway and the grass yard that had been planted in front of our house. Dressed in a light blue hooded parka and matching snow pants, I scrunched my mittened hands together. I had sloshed down our freshly shoveled sidewalk in my new rubber snow boots. Wisps of my sandy-blonde hair peeked out from under my fur hood, framing my green almond eyes and small freckled nose.

A smile of pure joy and delight spread across my four-year-old face. I had never seen snow before! Only in books, titled *Snow*, written in Dr. Seuss-style and simple language. But this was real snow, not a picture book version. The snow was whiter than sugar. It sparkled in the sunlight. The wet sidewalk glistened as I lifted and lowered my feet across the cement. I was not used to wearing snow boots. I maneuvered as best I could. Walking was tricky, but I was a determined little girl. Spunky, yet timid.

I posed on the sidewalk as daddy took pictures of me and mommy. We were happy! Mommy was pregnant. Her jacket, buttoned over her burgeoning belly hid the inevitable mystery. Smiling, we held hands. I felt loved. Not yet betrayed.

In spite of my cold nose and cheeks, I felt warm inside. Excited! I sensed the beauty and newness of the moment. We were a threesome—"Mommy-la," "Daddy-la," and "Pammy-la." This was our world. In the whiteness of the snow, our red bricked house stood out. Surrounded. A fortress all our own. Built just for us.

My little brother arrived in January. He was born using the Bradley natural method. My mother chose not to take pain medicine. In pictures that daddy took of the "amazing" birth, mommy looked very red-faced and disheveled. No make-up, her hair was not "done," but she was smiling. A real smile. The smile that I rarely saw. She had a beautiful smile with a sweet dimple in her cheek that would magically appear. I longed for her to smile that way at me.

DADDY & ME

At first, daddy didn't seem to mind my little brother's birth and how much time mommy spent taking care of the baby. I didn't mind either, except when I listened to her tell the baby every day how much she loved him,

"Hi, sweetheart! How's my little boy? I love you so much!" It seemed like she loved my little brother more than she loved us.

One night, not long after my little brother came home from the hospital, I woke up and heard mommy and daddy talking. Their voices were soft at first, like whispers, but then they started talking louder and louder. Mommy's voice was the loudest.

Sneaking out from under my covers, I decided to investigate. Very quietly, I opened my bedroom door and tiptoed down the hallway. Stopping right before I reached the living room, I peeked around the corner. Mommy and daddy were sitting on the turquoise-colored couch mommy had bought for our new house. They were both smoking cigarettes. Mommy was dressed in her light blue nightgown, the one you could see through. Daddy was wearing just his white t-shirt and black pants. He still had on his black socks.

"Well, Paul," I heard mommy yell at daddy, "I'll tell you why I didn't get my Clear Bracelet in D.C. I had a baby, remember? And I was working all the time, remember? I told you then I couldn't do both."

I watched from my hiding spot as mommy stood up, then paced back and forth in front of daddy, pointing her half-smoked cigarette dangerously close to his face. I worried that mommy might burn him. But daddy just sat there and stared at her. He didn't look mad or sad.

Finally, in a calm voice he said, "Gloria, sit down in that chair."

Instantly, mommy stopped pacing and turned her whole body toward daddy. As she bent down, her face got closer and closer to daddy's face. Her eyes and mouth opened wide, making her look scary, almost like a monster.

Wagging her lit cigarette in the air as she spoke, she yelled, "Don't use that shitty Communication Course command on me."

Daddy just sat there, staring back at her, repeating the same command, in the same calm voice, "Gloria, sit down in that chair." He sounded like a robot.

That did it! Mommy's body jerked as she stood up straight. Towering over daddy, she put her cigarette in her mouth and breathed in deeply. After forcefully letting out a large gray puff of air, she started laughing, like someone had told her something funny.

"Ha! That's a good one, Paul. You think you can control me, just because you're Clear!" Mommy had stopped laughing and started pointing her cigarette at daddy again.

A black ashtray sat on the coffee table in front of them. Mommy bent down and reached for it. Daddy tried to grab her wrist, but she moved too quickly. Picking up the ashtray she hurled it at him, covering him with gray ashes and cigarette butts. Laughing even louder now, she turned and walked toward the kitchen.

Daddy stood up. After carefully dusting the contents of the ashtray off his shirt and pants, I watched him follow mommy into the kitchen, while the expression on his face never changed. Very quietly, I tiptoed back to my bedroom. Without making a sound, I shut the door behind me. As I climbed back into bed, I thought about what I'd just seen. Why was mommy so mad? Why did she try to hurt daddy when all he did was tell her to sit down?

• • •

"The seven-year-old girl who shudders because a man kisses her
is not computing; she is reacting to an engram since at seven
she should see nothing wrong in a kiss, not even a passionate one."

– L. Ron Hubbard,
Dianetics: The Modern Science of Mental Health, 1950

Mommy always spent so long putting my little baby brother to bed, daddy decided he'd be in charge of me. I heard him tell mommy that he knew it was hard for her to handle everything, so he'd take care of me.

At bedtime, I loved hearing my favorite stories read to me. But daddy didn't really like reading stories the way mommy did. Mostly, daddy just liked to sit on my bed and talk. Sometimes he'd ask me funny things. Not funny like a joke or a silly story, but funny things that I'd never really heard mommy, or our neighbors, or even my teacher ask.

One night, while daddy and I sat next to each other on the pink bedspread that covered my new canopy bed, he asked me, "Pammy, do you like to be kissed?"

I was surprised that daddy would ask me about kissing, because we weren't much of a kissing family. Usually, I just held hands with mommy or daddy, like when we were walking down the street or inside a store. Sometimes, but not often, mommy might give me a goodnight kiss on my forehead, which I did like, so I told daddy, "Yes." Daddy smiled and moved a little closer to me.

The next night, after I took a bath and put on my pajamas I walked into my bedroom and saw daddy sitting on my bed. He told me to come and sit next to him, then he closed the door. Looking serious, he told me we needed to be quiet because mommy was putting the baby to bed.

I said, "OK. I can be very quiet. As quiet as a mouse."

Usually, mommy and daddy smiled when I said that, but this time daddy didn't smile. He looked sad, and even a little mad.

Then he asked me, in a softer kind of voice, "Do you want to play a game?" I liked games like hide-and-seek, and dress-up with my dolls, and even games like checkers, so I said, "Yes." Daddy looked happy, so I was happy.

Then daddy told me, in an even quieter kind of voice, not a whisper, but a voice that was much quieter than his usual daddy voice, "OK. We're going to play Mommy and Daddy."

That sounded like a good game to me. We'd never played it before, but I wanted to play. And it was nice to have daddy all to myself, alone in my room, without mommy, who was always holding and cuddling my baby brother.

At night, and sometimes two nights in a row, daddy came into my bedroom, but only when mommy went to take a bath and wash her hair, after putting the baby to bed. With the door closed, he sat next to me on my small bed and reminded me that we needed to be very quiet, because the baby was sleeping.

Daddy told me to lie down on my tummy. I felt his hands rub the top of my back, my legs, and then my bottom. As he touched my body, he told me this was part of the Mommy and Daddy game. I felt excited about playing a game only daddy and I knew how to play, and it felt nice when he put his warm hand on my leg.

One time, while we played our game, Daddy even kissed me. He put his mouth on my lips and told me that he and mommy liked to kiss like that, which made me feel special, and glad that daddy wanted to kiss me, too.

After daddy left, I fell asleep, but soon woke up when I heard footsteps outside my bedroom. It sounded like both mommy and daddy were walking in the hallway.

"Paul," I heard mommy tell daddy, "I'm exhausted. It's only been two months since the baby. It's too soon."

"I'm tired of that excuse, Gloria." Daddy's voice sounded angry.

I sat up in bed and listened as mommy told daddy, "Paul, stop, please. That hurts."

"Listen, Gloria, it's been long enough. Since before the baby. Our second dynamic is out. You know as well as I do, sex is necessary for survival. Do you need to reread the eight dynamics? No? Well, let me remind you what Ron said, 'It's the greatest good for the greatest number of dynamics.'"

I wasn't sure what daddy was talking about, but I did know he sounded very angry at mommy. I guessed they were talking about Scientology, which always seemed to make them mad at each other.

Pulling the covers up a little closer to my face, I wondered if mommy was going to throw something at daddy again. I thought about getting out of bed to peek at them, but I was too afraid mommy would get mad at me. I didn't want her to throw any cigarettes on me like she did to daddy.

As mommy and daddy's voices got quieter, it was hard to hear what they were saying. Then I heard mommy crying. She sounded very sad.

"I'm sorry, Paul," I heard her tell daddy, in between sobs. "I know. I've been withholding from you. I was just reacting from the birth." Mommy stopped talking and blew her nose loudly.

"Gloria," daddy answered her in his robot-like voice, "I acknowledge your withhold." Then daddy told her, "Let's go to bed."

I was glad mommy hadn't yelled at daddy, or thrown anything at him. Even though she was crying, I hoped she'd do whatever daddy told her, so he'd be happy. Then I stretched out in my bed and tucked the covers carefully under my chin before closing my eyes and falling back to sleep.

. . .

As we lay naked underneath the pink quilted bedspread, this night felt different. Daddy had undone his belt buckle and pulled his black pants and white underwear off, leaving on only his black socks. His touch was stronger and harder as he rubbed his hands over my bare bottom. It didn't hurt, but it felt mad, like when you push hard against a door to make it open, or pull on a drawer that is stuck. It seemed like daddy couldn't wait as he moved his hands faster and faster over my body, like he was in a hurry.

Afterward, sitting in his lap, daddy looked down at me. His voice became serious, and he sounded worried as he explained, "Remember, this is our special game. Only you and I can play this game. Mommy and the baby don't know how to play, and they wouldn't understand the game. Mommy might even get mad if we told her about it. This is our secret."

Well, that convinced me. No one wanted to listen to mommy when she was mad. Not daddy, not my baby brother, and definitely not me. I hated when mommy yelled. Worse was when she threw things, especially at daddy. Why did she get so mad? Laying in my bed, after daddy left, I thought about what he told me. We needed to keep our "game" a secret. Mommy wouldn't like it.

The next time we played our "Mommy and Daddy Game,"

daddy and I were alone. Mommy was not home. The room was dark, and it was warm under the covers. Lying side by side in my bed, my small naked body next to his, our skin touched in the middle. My tiny hands were overpowered by his as he moved them up and down the hard part of his body that was underneath his large, squishy belly. Feeling the pressure of his hands on mine, I learned it's all consensual when you're four years old.

Abruptly, daddy sat up and moved my hands away. Completely covered by sheets and a blanket, we heard only muffled sounds outside my bedroom before the door opened.

"What are you doing in here?" I heard mommy's voice ask, as I emerged from under the covers. My small face peeked out next to daddy's bare chest.

"Get out!" mommy screamed. "Get out of her bed! What the hell are you doing?"

Daddy stood up and bent down to reach his black pants and white underwear that were lying in a pile on the hardwood floor next to the bed. I watched the black hair on the back of his head as he moved. His neck was bright red. Next to the blackness of his hair, it looked like someone had poured ketchup on his neck.

I peeked across the room and saw mommy standing in the doorway. She was dressed in a white blouse with black slacks. She looked at me. I felt her rage penetrate through my skin. Then she turned and followed daddy, who had dressed and walked out into the hall. Using all her strength, she grabbed the doorknob and loudly slammed my bedroom door shut.

I heard their footsteps in the hallway. Then I heard mommy yelling. Her words were hard to hear, but the pitch and tone were familiar. Harsh, angry, unrelenting. I lay under the sheets and the blanket, naked, scared, and alone.

. . .

But even though mommy had been so mad, it seemed like she forgot about what happened, and daddy's nightly visits continued, although they became even more secretive.

Conveniently close, my bedroom was right next to my parents' bedroom. My ears became trained to listen for the almost silent sound of their bedroom door closing behind daddy before he entered my room. Mommy must not have heard it because she was too tired.

I wondered if she was still mad at daddy and me. I didn't hear them yelling at night anymore, but sometimes, when she thought I didn't see her, mommy would look at me in a mean way, like she was still angry.

Uninterrupted by the quietness of the house, daddy's large hands moved over me. In the darkness, I could make out the outline of the swaying silhouette above my head. I watched carefully as the pink ruffle, hanging from the top of my white canopy bed, moved rhythmically back and forth. My pink pajamas felt silky, soft, and smooth on my small arms, while the edge of daddy's silver wedding band felt hard and rough as it rubbed against my bare skin.

Abruptly, the canopy ruffle fluttered and then stopped, suddenly still. The bedroom door opened, just enough to let in a sliver of light from the hallway, and then soundlessly closed. It was dark again.

As if it never happened. I pulled on my white cotton underwear and silky pink pajama bottoms. My white blanket felt soft around my face, but the pillow sham, that matched my pink ruffled bedspread, was scratchy against my cheek. I lay very still, like a statue that had just been placed in a dark museum corner at night. Lifeless, cold, and void of feeling. Lying in the dark, I closed my eyes and fell asleep.

SIX YEARS
OLD

Seated on the rug in front of the brick fireplace, I straddled my little brother and held him tightly around the waist. His small hands grasped the large book, *The Night Before Christmas.* The classic version by Clemens. Wearing a white shirt and black pants, his thick dark brown, really, almost black baby hair was parted to the side and slicked down with Brill Cream, the hair product of the '50s and '60s.

As daddy crouched down to take the pictures, he told us to smile. I looked at him as I held my little brother. But even though it was almost time for Christmas, I didn't feel happy, and I refused to smile. Daddy clicked the button on the camera. My little brother and I both blinked.

Mommy stood behind daddy and tried to make us smile. "Come on kids, show me your smiles," she coaxed as she showed us her own dimpled smile.

Daddy tried again, clicking several more pictures. Finally, he turned to mommy and said, "Gloria, I think that's enough. I'm sure there's at least one where they're smiling." I knew daddy loved to take pictures. I was surprised that he didn't want to take more.

Later, when the pictures were developed, mommy laid them out on the kitchen table and looked carefully at each one. I wasn't smiling in any of them. But my little brother was either smiling, laughing, or closing his eyes. He looked sweet, young, and innocent. I looked sad and resigned.

I watched mommy as she picked up each of the photographs. Holding them up to the kitchen light, she studied them closely, intent on choosing the perfect Christmas card picture.

Turning toward me, as I watched from a distance, she asked, "Pammy, why didn't you smile when daddy took the pictures? I can't find even one where both of you are smiling."

I looked at her and thought, I didn't smile because I didn't want to, especially not for you. I put my head down and walked out of the room, knowing I'd disappointed mommy, again.

The Christmas card picture she finally chose hung on a red ribbon over the brick fireplace mantle, with all the other Christmas cards that arrived in the mail. When mommy wasn't watching, I stood on my tiptoes and stared at it, wondering why she picked it. I also wondered if she knew that daddy and I still played our secret "game."

. . .

It was a winter day, after Christmas. There was snow on the ground. A small dusting of two to three inches. Just enough to play in. My little brother and I put on our snowsuits. My new snowsuit was light pink. Sitting on the brick steps that led to our small front porch, I helped him put on his mittens and his boots before I put on my own. Fur hood pulled over my hair, we walked down the steps to our snow-covered front lawn.

I laid down and felt the cold snow surround my arms, legs, and head. I closed my eyes tightly, then opened them to see the sky. It was a brilliant clear blue. Cloudless. Perfect. I moved my arms and legs vigorously up and down, from side to side, making a snow angel. For a moment, I felt free.

Later that same year, sitting atop the metal jungle gym in our backyard, surrounded by a newly erected unpainted wooden fence, I felt the hard gray bars, warmed by the September sun against my hands. Standing up, I pushed my sneakered feet down on the bars below me.

Craning my neck, I could see over the wooden fence to the yard behind ours. The grass was green and perfectly mowed, just like our backyard. Tabletop Mountain stood out in the distance, like a giant wall behind the yard and the houses at the end of the block.

Mommy told me and my little brother it was named that because it was very flat at the top, just like a table. Staring up at the mountain, it seemed big and scary next to our red brick house with white trim, the answer to mommy's dream to live in 1960s suburbia.

Although just six years old, I imagined myself already an adult. My innocence had been taken away from me, slowly and methodically, through a series of purposeful violations. My state of mind was one of sadness and worry. It felt like thick dense fog enveloping the landscape. Heavy and blinding.

Climbing off my private playground, I felt despondent, alone, and afraid. Of what? I didn't know, but I felt it. Etched deep within my thoughts, my small body, and my red brick house, secret words and deeds were hidden. As I reached out to touch the gray metal bar next to me, it felt solid and supportive. Dependable. The antithesis of my parents.

. . .

Unexpectedly, one spring morning, mommy told me we were moving. I was both surprised and angry. I loved my school near Denver, Colorado and my teacher who'd taught me how to read Dr. Seuss books.

Feeling bold, I decided to fight back by telling mommy I wanted to change my name. If I was moving, this was my chance to become someone else.

As I told her my plan, she looked at me, somewhat puzzled, and asked, "So, Pammy, what do you want your name to be?"

Surprised by the fact that she was even honoring my request, I confidently stated, "I don't know, but not Pammy or Pamela."

Amused, she entertained the conversation and said, "Well, you could change your name to Suzanne, your middle name."

Hmm, I thought. Would that work? I asked her, "How?"

With a somewhat sincere look on her face, she took a drag of her cigarette and replied, "Well, when you meet new friends at school, tell them your name is Suzanne. Then they'll call you Suzanne."

So easy! Except for one minor problem, all my school records would have my real name, my legal name, on them. But, at six years old, I had no idea how the world really worked. I was just a child, immersed in an adult world that I really didn't understand.

So, quite effortlessly, mommy tricked me into thinking I might actually be able to change my name, and become a new person. In my mind, one that was separate, in a sense, from my parents and my family. If I was Suzanne, I could reinvent myself. This became both my fantasy and my wish. I even practiced writing Suzanne, instead of Pammy, to see how it looked. It was two extra letters, but I was a good speller, and I knew how to write them all.

SLIDELL, LOUISIANA, CIRCA 1964

Of course, when mommy enrolled me in second grade in Slidell, Louisiana, after our summer move, my teacher called me Pamela. The name I detested. Only mommy called me Pamela, especially when she was angry with me for having done something she didn't like, which seemed often.

Leaving Colorado had been hard, especially for me and daddy. One day, before we left, mommy, daddy, me, and my little brother all went to visit Millie and John. Their house wasn't far from where we lived. When we got out of the car, Millie greeted us, giving both my parents a big hug.

Then she bent down so she was eye level with me and my little brother. "Look at you!" she exclaimed. "You've gotten so big!"

As she stood up, Mike, her son, who was about the same age as I was, but much taller, came over and stood next to her.

"Look," she told him, "The Nickels are here." Putting her hand on my small shoulder, she told him, "This is Pammy. Why don't you go play in the backyard while Gloria and Paul come inside to talk to Dad."

Mike smiled and said, "Okay." He led us around the house to the green grass that stretched out behind it where I immediately saw the swing set. It was just like the one in our backyard. I ran toward it and jumped up onto a swing. Mike sat down in the other swing next to me. My little brother followed us, but decided to play with the toy truck he'd brought from home. He zoomed it around in the dirt near the swing set while Mike and I pumped our legs, swinging higher and higher.

Both mommy and daddy followed Millie into the house. I never saw John, or daddy again, until we left. After a while, Millie opened the back door of the house. She walked outside and sat down in the shade underneath a tree. Mommy came out next and sat down beside her. Still swinging, I watched them as they talked and smoked.

Their backyard was not quite as big as our yard, so the swing set was not too far from where they sat. In between puffs of their cigarettes, I heard Millie tell mommy, "John and I both miss D.C. It was a privilege to work for Ron. But now, he and Mary Sue are at Saint Hill. We need to keep disseminating Scientology in the States."

She paused for a minute, then added, "And John's been trying out some new tech here."

My ears perked up a little when I heard Millie talking about Scientology. Not quite seven years old, I'd begun to feel somewhat curious about it. But Mike, who was still sitting in the swing next to me, seemed oblivious to their conversation, and paid no attention to them.

Perched on my swing, I watched mommy as she listened to Millie. She didn't say anything. She just nodded her head, and puffed on her cigarette, which was now mostly smoked, except for a small butt that she held between her fingers. I knew that soon, she'd reach into her pocket, take out another one, light it up, and continue smoking. I'd watched her smoke cigarette after cigarette many times.

Millie continued, "It's a shame you and Paul are leaving. I get the money end of it, but what are YOU going to do in Louisiana?"

It sounded like Millie was worried about mommy.

Mommy sat quietly, smoking and staring at my little brother, who was still playing in the dirt. Millie kept talking. "There aren't any franchises in New Orleans. I know the Hancocks are planning on going to Saint Hill. Maybe they'll open one when they get back."

Mommy stared at Millie for a second, then answered her, "Yes, maybe. I'm not sure. But Paul and I both acknowledged this is a good opportunity. He'll work for a bigger company, and make more money."

I'd learned, by listening to mommy and daddy argue, that the word acknowledged meant that you agreed. But I wasn't sure if daddy had agreed to the move, or if it was really just mommy's idea.

Mommy stopped talking, just long enough to put her cigarette to her lips. As she blew out the smoke, she explained, "We've talked about going to Saint Hill. Maybe when the kids are a little older though."

Millie looked at mommy. Her voice sounded serious now, "Gloria, haven't you read *The Auditor*? Power Processing is happening at Saint Hill. Now's the time to go!

I'd never heard mommy talk about going to Saint Hill before. I wondered where it was, and if we'd move there next.

As if it was planned, the back door of the house opened and daddy and John walked out. Daddy was smiling. Mike and I jumped off our swings, and ran toward them. Mike reached his dad first. I tried to keep up with him as he ran, but I wasn't as fast. When I finally reached daddy, he scooped me up in his arms and asked me what I was doing. I told him we were swinging, but not that I'd been listening to mommy and Millie.

As we all walked together toward the front of the house, I heard John say somewhat quietly to Millie, "Paul's dealing with some heavy stuff. His case needs some handling."

I had no idea what that meant, but John sounded worried about daddy.

Millie frowned and replied, "We talked about Saint Hill, but I'm not sure what they're going to do."

Mommy and daddy were unusually quiet on the drive home. Mommy just stared out the window while my little brother fell asleep next to me. Not wanting to wake him, I sat quiet and still in the back seat, listening to the only sound in the car, the rhythmic clink of daddy's Clear Bracelet as it brushed against the steering wheel.

• • •

Mommy told me we moved to Slidell, a suburb of New Orleans, just across the Pontchartrain Bridge, for daddy's new job. When I asked her what kind of job, she told me daddy was a technical writer, and there were lots of new jobs for people who wrote manuals about how things worked.

She told me he was going to work for a company called Lockheed Martin where they built rockets that were going to go into outer space. Writing manuals, whatever those were, didn't sound fun, but building rockets seemed exciting. I wondered if daddy would be able to watch them being built, or maybe even ride in one.

Shortly after we moved, Hurricane Betsy hit New Orleans. My parents had never experienced a hurricane before. Thunderstorms were common in the Midwest, and even tornadoes, but not hurricanes.

I looked down the street as mommy and our next-door neighbor jokingly talked about securing everything down for the storm. The sky was gray, almost black. You could barely see the houses at the end of the block. It felt eerie, like a scary movie.

As they laughed, it seemed like mommy was nervous. I watched her as she fiddled to find her cigarettes in her purse. Mommy smoked a lot, even more than daddy. As mommy looked for her cigarettes, the neighbor teased her about the car being secured in a cupboard in our garage. I wasn't sure if she was joking, or making fun of mommy. It seemed like she didn't really like mommy, and was just pretending to be nice.

Daddy had taken the car to run a last-minute errand to get batteries for the transistor radio. It was our only way to hear news of the storm if, and when, the power went out. The rain started after dinner, hard rain. You could hear it on the roof and the windows. We all sat on the couch in the living room, which we never did as a family.

Daddy held the black battery-powered transistor radio in

his hand and turned up the volume. We listened to the weather report telling us where the eye of the storm was moving. I didn't understand how a storm could have an eye, but I didn't ask. I was too scared.

My little brother sat next to mommy on the couch, snuggled in tight, dressed in his Superman pajamas, cape, and all, clutching his Superman action figure tightly in his little hands. Water started to pound harder on the roof and then on the front door. I turned to look at the door and saw water starting to come in. I was worried the water might keep coming in, and fill up our house, and that I might drown. I didn't know how to swim.

Mommy got up and walked to the door. She was barefoot. I could hear the water squishing under her toes as it slowly soaked into the green shag carpet. She looked worried. Then she walked back and sat down on the couch. Seated on the other end, ignoring the three of us, daddy held the transistor radio in the palm of his hand. Looking straight ahead, his face was void of emotion. If he was worried, he didn't show it.

Sitting next to mommy, tired and scared, I decided to lie down. She covered me with a blanket. I think I dozed in and out of sleep, intermittently hearing the transistor radio as it provided hurricane updates in the distance. It reported that the eye of the storm was somewhere nearby, but not too close. My eyes were closed when I felt mommy lift me up, and carry me to my bedroom.

Feeling her arms under me, I relaxed and went limp, like I could fall fast asleep. But as soon as she laid me down on top of the covers on my bed, a pine needle flew against the window. The sound was quick and sharp. It sounded like cracking glass. Mommy looked at the window, scooped me up, and quickly carried me back to the living room couch.

The hurricane caused severe damage and destruction in New Orleans, but Slidell escaped the worst, with mostly minor flood damage, like what happened to our house. But my parents decided not to spend the insurance money on repairs. Instead, mommy hired a contractor, named Joe, to help her design our new house. I could tell that mommy liked Joe.

She seemed to enjoy listening to him as he told her about the plans for the house in his thick Southern drawl. I thought he looked like a very tall cowboy. He even sounded like one. I visited the new house with mommy a few times before it was finished. She liked to walk around the courtyard, entering through the black wrought iron gate she'd picked out. I heard her tell Joe how she wanted the entrance to have a "Southern, New Orleans feel" to it. I watched mommy smile as she closed the gate behind us. She seemed happy.

As soon as the house was ready, we quickly moved in. Mommy kept some of the furniture from our old house, like the white Formica kitchen table with chrome legs and little gray specks on it, along with the turquoise blue faux leather couch we sat on in the family room.

The other furniture that mommy bought for the new house was expensive top-of-the-line from Ethan Allen. She loved the look of pecan wood, and ordered a dining room table with matching wood chairs that had avocado green velvet seats.

A matching avocado green sofa, with the same pecan finished wood accents, and gold velvet chairs were also purchased, followed by daddy's most prized possession, a state-of-the-art 1960s console wood stereo, pecan finished as well. Mommy seemed to love decorating!

Our living room and dining room resembled a page out of a 1965 edition of *Better Homes & Gardens*.

Living in Slidell, just outside of New Orleans, made it easy to visit. On Sundays, mommy and daddy liked to drive across the Pontchartrain Bridge into the city. I loved driving over the bridge! You could see water on both sides. Daddy told me we were driving over part of the Gulf of Mexico, which sounded like the name of a country I'd heard of.

On this Sunday, we'd just returned from brunch at the Court of Two Sisters restaurant in Jackson Square in New Orleans. I wore an olive green jumper and a print blouse that mommy had made for me. My little brother and I posed in front of our new house while daddy took our picture.

I smiled, a somewhat toothless grin, as I'd just lost my two front teeth. I felt happy. At our feet sat our new puppy, Blackie. Soft and fluffy, she was sweet and docile. Not a jumpy or barky dog. I loved her!

While we were in New Orleans, daddy had taken pictures of mommy in front of the statue of Andrew Jackson on his horse. Tall and slim with reddish-brown hair, elegant and sophisticated, she looked a little like Jackie Kennedy. Dressed in an olive green suit jacket and matching skirt, black sunglasses and a matching handbag, with dark pumps on her narrow size AA feet, mommy looked happy and beautiful. In that moment, no evidence of her Scientology life existed.

SOUTHERN
SUBURBIA

Herb Albert & the Tijuana Brass blasted from the speakers as the vinyl record spun at thirty-three miles-per-hour on the turntable.

"Be careful," daddy warned. "Here, let me show you."

Using his thumb and index finger, in the same way mommy used her index finger and middle finger to hold her Kool cigarette, daddy pulled out the white paper cover that held the black disc.

"You never want to touch the record, or you'll scratch it."

I watched as daddy loosened the record from the white paper. Then he stuck his index finger in the center hole, surrounded by the red label, and pushed it ever so slightly. Just the edge of the black circle peeked out.

"See?" Daddy said as he showed me how to hold the record.

Then he added, speaking very seriously, "You don't want to scratch or smudge the record. Scratches cause skips. Then the record's ruined."

His serious tone meant that a scratch on any of his records could constitute a rule infraction that might require some form of punishment or retribution. I wasn't sure what he might do, but I was certain that I didn't want to find out and suffer any consequences. Being compliant had become second nature.

Daddy carefully pulled the record from the white paper and placed it on the turntable. I gingerly lifted the head of the needle and lightly placed it on the first groove of the large record, following his precise directions.

Dancing around the living room, pretending to blow an imaginary horn, just like the players on the record cover, I felt grown up. Not grown up with responsibilities, but grown up in a physical and sensual way. Listening to the bluesy jazz with a man, my daddy, watching me while I swayed and moved to the music stirred something inside me. It felt warm, almost loving. I watched him as he smoked a cigarette, smiling at me and tapping his fingers on the arm of the gold velvet chair.

Daddy wasn't a small man, and his body filled the entire space of the chair, from one side of the gold velvet cushion to the other. The gold piping around the edges of the seat were covered by his large bottom and thick thighs. As he tapped his black socked foot against the green shag carpet, keeping beat with the music, I looked up at him.

We made eye contact, for an instant, before I quickly looked down again. In that moment, somewhere between the signature sound of the brass horn and the melodic deep tones of the saxophone, my seven-year-old body felt sexual, warm, and inviting. But daddy didn't touch me, or say anything. Our secret was unspoken, but the truth could be seen in his eyes.

Not long after we moved into our newly built house, daddy's bedroom visits continued. I imagined myself special and important when I thought about our secret. We shared something that mommy and my little brother didn't know about. Or if mommy did know, she pretended she didn't. Conflicted, I felt angry, unloved, and abandoned by her.

. . .

On a rainy day at my new school, where I didn't have many friends, valentines were being delivered in little white bags decorated with hearts and doilies. Suddenly, I needed to go to the bathroom. I felt it coming out. I couldn't stop it.

I walked around the classroom, wondering who knew. I was afraid to tell anyone, especially my new teacher, Mrs. Tarnack, who seemed mean and unapproachable. I smelled bad, so I stood next to the classroom window, staring at the rain dripping down the windowpane. I watched as the water fell, dropping on the pine trees, and covering the sidewalk outside, turning it a shinier shade of ugly gray.

At the end of the school day, instead of walking home, mommy picked me up in the car because it was raining. As soon as I got in, she asked me what smelled. I didn't answer. We drove home in silence. When we got inside our house, she touched my bottom and looked into my red tights, where she saw brown poo oozing over the top of the waistband.

"Pamela Suzanne!" she spoke in a sharp tone, "Why didn't you tell me?"

Always my full given name when she was angry. I put my head

down, and said nothing. Then she led me into the bathroom. She told me to stand in the bathtub and take off my red jumper and white blouse. I lifted my jumper and pulled it over my head. Then I unbuttoned my blouse and pulled my arms out.

She took my clothes from me, then carefully pulled my red tights down to my ankles. I stepped out of them and sat down in the cold, hard tub. Turning on the warm water, she carefully washed away the remnants of feces from my bottom and my legs. She even put some bubble bath, Mr. Bubble, in the tub and let me soak in the pink. It smelled good, even comforting.

I didn't know this tender, caring side of mommy. She seemed nice, even kind. I was wary, unsure, waiting for an angry explosion. But she didn't yell. She left me in the tub to soak a little longer. I was just a little girl, with two missing front teeth, sandy-blonde shoulder-length hair, beautiful green eyes, and a smattering of freckles, sitting in a tub full of sweet-smelling bubbles on a rainy Valentine's Day. A bag full of red, pink, and white valentine cards filled with candy hearts waited for me when I got out. I should've been happy.

But I didn't trust happiness, and I didn't trust mommy and daddy. They were volatile, strange adults. I wondered, always, what it would be like to live with different parents. I daydreamed often about living at our neighbor's house.

The bubbles smelled good. I scooped up a handful and blew them onto the side of the bathtub. They stuck there for a moment and then slid back into the tub. Mommy came back to check on me and asked me if I was clean. I nodded and stood up in the tub, letting the bubbles slowly slip down my legs. She wrapped me in a warm towel and lifted me out of the tub. I stood on the bathmat as she dried me off.

For a moment, her arms felt comforting on the other side of the towel. Then, stiffening against her touch, I couldn't let myself feel consoled. This tenderness was unusual. Her love felt unpredictable. I looked up at her and asked if I could go play with my Barbies in my room. She looked down at me with a strange expression on her face, and told me to put on my pajamas.

Sadly, I walked to my bedroom, wrapped in the warm towel. My feet were slightly damp, and there were still a few traces of white bubbles around my toes. I bent down and touched the airy, wet circles, popping them with my index finger. Standing in my bedroom, my dolls waited for me. Perfectly poised on my shelf, dressed, and groomed. They were reliable, always there. My Barbies wouldn't betray me. Their presence made me feel safe.

❈

SUMMER MEMORIES, CIRCA 1965

It was July in Louisiana, and the weather was hot, humid, and sticky. If the mosquitos didn't get to you, then the wasps would. The mud nest had been built by the wasp family, probably the mother wasp, to fit precisely inside the V-shaped metal opening at the top of the red-painted poles that held our swing set in place.

Carelessly, the poles hadn't been cemented into the ground, and they lifted up each time my little brother or I swung too high, which was pretty much every time. We sat in the plastic blue swings and pumped our legs, propelling ourselves slightly higher than the dirt and grass ground that the swing set sat on.

Jumping off the swings, my little brother and I walked to the cement walkway that led to the front door, next to the carport, not really a garage, but more like an enclosed room for the car. The walkway stopped at the dirt and mostly weeds, which daddy liked to call grass, which was rarely watered because there wasn't a sprinkler system.

Occasionally, mommy would screw the green hose to the metal sprinkler, which had tiny holes in it that sprayed out water, and let my little brother and I run in the small streams of liquid that it produced. This usually happened in the front yard though, where the grass was greener. After running around in the sprinkler, tired and a little bored, my little brother and I sat down on the curb in front of the house, playing in the mud we'd made from the dirt and runoff from the sprinkler.

Hands covered in brown dirt and dark mud, we pretended to have an elaborate bakery assembly line in the gutter in front of our house. My little brother would form the chocolate-colored mud balls. Then I'd roll them in the lighter cocoa-colored dirt and place them carefully on the curb, as if placing them in a bakery window for display. This kept us busy for a while.

Soon tiring of this game, we decided to go play in the backyard, just about the same time that daddy decided to start mowing. The whir of the mower could be heard from the front yard. We walked along the driveway through the wrought iron gate that led to the cement path, past the front door and the carport, to the backyard. My little brother and I stood on the cement in our bare feet and bathing suits, watching as daddy mowed the dirt underneath the swing set.

As daddy pushed the mower under the long red metal bar that held the chains of the swings, wasps started flying frantically above daddy's head. There were at least a dozen wasps diving and dipping down, buzzing around daddy's ears, and flying frighteningly close to his face.

As loudly as I could, I screamed, "Bees!" But daddy just kept mowing as if he couldn't see or hear them, or me. I yelled again as loudly as I could, "Daddy! Watch out! Bees!"

Waving my hands frantically, I tried to get his attention. But he just continued to push the mower back and forth underneath the swing set, dangerously close to the wasps and their mud nest. Seeking safety, my little brother had already run inside to hide from the wasps, and to get a snack. I left daddy and hurried after him to tell mommy about the bees.

Mommy was in the kitchen, cigarette in hand, poised over a cookbook. She was always trying out new recipes for daddy. Cakes were his favorite. Mommy made daddy a cake almost every week because he ate them so fast.

My little brother stood near the refrigerator, soda in hand, asking mommy if he could have some cookies. Barely looking up from her cookbook, she opened the cupboard door and placed five black-and-white Oreos in the palm of his small dirty hand. Then she took a drag on her cigarette and looked up to see me standing in the doorway between the kitchen and the family room.

From inside the house, you could no longer hear the whir of the lawnmower. Daddy had stopped mowing and come inside behind me. He was red-faced and dripping with sweat.

Mommy looked right past me at daddy and asked, "Paul, are you done mowing?"

"Yeah, it's pretty hot out there," he answered as he walked past me toward the kitchen. "I need some water," he panted.

I looked at daddy. I wanted to tell him how I'd tried to save him from the bees. But he was too busy drinking a glass of water that mommy had filled up for him from the kitchen faucet. Then he sat down at the kitchen table and wiped the sweat off his face with a kitchen towel that mommy had handed him.

As she started telling him about a new recipe she was going to try out, I realized both mommy and daddy weren't going to listen to me. Feeling invisible, unimportant, and dejected, I put my head down, walked down the hall, went in my bedroom, and shut the door.

Sitting cross-legged on the green shag carpet, I carefully placed Barbie, Midge, Ken, and Skipper into their respective rooms in my vinyl Barbie Dreamhouse. It was the kind that folded up neatly into a suitcase, so Barbie and her friends could be easily transported, although I never took them anywhere.

As I sat there, holding my Barbie, dressed in her colorful Peter Max-inspired minidress, I thought about wanting to be a different kind of little girl. The kind that mommies and daddies love the right way. I didn't understand why daddy didn't thank me for warning him about the bees. For saving him. Didn't I help him when he needed me?

• • •

Later that summer, on a very hot and humid morning, mommy chose to venture outside to the patch of dirt just outside our kitchen door, where she tended a small garden. She grew tomatoes, along with succulents and plants native to the hot and humid southern climate of Louisiana.

My little brother and I were already outside, standing in the vacant lot next to our house, entertaining ourselves with pine tree branches and a large muddy puddle of mosquito-infested water. We enjoyed dipping the sticky branches in the brown water, swirling them around, and watching the mosquitoes as they swarmed.

After a while, hot and tired of playing this game, I looked over toward our house. I watched mommy as she picked a green tomato off one of the vines on the tomato plant. She held it in the palm of her hand and inspected it, then wiped it off on the cotton sleeve of her white blouse. Holding it firmly in one hand, she brought it to her lips, opened her mouth, and bit into it. As she chewed the green tomato, seeds and all, she looked over at me and my little brother.

Our eyes locked. I couldn't hide my disgust for mommy, and for her behavior. It was written all over my face.

Casually, she asked, "What's wrong? Haven't you ever seen me eat a tomato before?"

I thought about her question for a second, and sheepishly replied, "Yes, but not like that."

Mommy looked at me curiously and responded, "Well, when I was a little girl...."

Here we go, I thought. Another one of her stories. They were always long and included too many details that made me think, like I did almost every day, that I wished she wasn't my mommy. I'm not sure why exactly. She just seemed so different from the other moms who picked up their kids from school. Those moms always seemed friendly, and acted the way I thought moms should.

Sometimes, after school, while I waited for mommy, I'd listen to the moms talking as they shared recipes and planned get-togethers. I often wished mommy could act more like them.

One day, when mommy picked me up from school, I watched the

other moms look at her oddly, as if she were something interesting to be watched, not dangerous, just different. Walking past them, on the way to our car, I overheard them talking.

"Do you know her? Someone told me they moved here from Colorado."

"I know she doesn't attend our church. I've never seen her there."

"She definitely isn't a Southerner. I doubt they stay here long."

I looked at mommy's face, but I wasn't sure if she'd been listening to them. In a way, I felt sorry for mommy. It didn't sound like they wanted to be friends with her. But she didn't really seem to be trying either.

Then suddenly, mommy stopped and turned her head to stare at them. Her eyes were unblinking, like she was in a trance or something. The moms were still talking, but they didn't seem to notice mommy staring at them. After a few seconds, she blinked, and continued walking to the car, without saying a word. Sadly, mommy didn't seem to know how to make friends.

Standing next to her tomato plant, mommy's story continued, "On our farm in Kansas, we'd eat the tomatoes straight off the vine, dousing them with salt. My brother, Bobby, always had a competition to see who could spit the most seeds out."

Then she added, "Of course, I always beat Bobby. Then he'd chase me through the garden and run inside to tell our mom how I'd picked her tomatoes before they were even ripe."

She'd stopped eating the green tomato to tell her story. Suddenly, in mid-sentence, mommy stopped talking all together, as if a new thought or purpose had entered her head. I'd watched her do this before.

Thoughtfully, she looked down at the half-eaten tomato in her hand and took another bite. Still chewing, she opened the side door of the house that led into the kitchen, went inside, and closed the door behind her.

I looked over at my little brother who was still busy swirling his pine tree branch in the muddy water. Mosquitoes buzzed around him as he swung the branch at them, making them swarm even more. He was being bitten and sucked dry, even though we'd both been sprayed with a thick coating of OFF Mosquito Repellant. Soon, he'd start itching and crying for mommy, who would cover him in a thick coating of pink Calamine Lotion.

But, for now, lost in her thoughts and in her own world, mommy had chosen safety inside our house, with her half-eaten tomato.

NEIGHBORHOOD
FRIENDS

A lyssa and I played Barbies in Davina's room upstairs. Davina was Alyssa's older sister, who at thirteen years old wore a bra and silky panties. Once when she was getting dressed, Alyssa and I opened the door and saw her in her underwear. Her white cotton bra held two young firm breasts. The white shiny panties covered her bottom and her tummy. Just the very top edge of her belly button peeked out from the elastic waistband of her smooth nylon panties.

When Davina saw us, Alyssa holding the gold-colored doorknob, and me peering in at her as I stood next to Alyssa, she shouted, "Alyssa, shut the door! I'm getting dressed. You never remember to knock."

Then she added, "I hate sharing a room with you. It's not fair!"

Alyssa smirked and shut the door.

"Come on!" she whispered, as I followed her up the short staircase to her older brothers' room.

The three boys shared the bedroom at the top of the house. The loft room was situated under the two top shuttered windows of the house. Built in 1965, the new two-story house was quite modern, yet Southern provincial. Red brick with white shutters. A large sliding glass door off the kitchen and family room led to a tree-lined backyard. Their kitchen was bigger and longer than ours, with a table for a family of seven, three boys and two girls, plus their mom and dad.

Alyssa's mother collected china and tea settings. They covered the tables in the living room, carefully placed on white lace doilies that adorned deep cherry wood side tables, buffets, and tea carts. We never walked into the living room. Instead, we entered the house through those sliding glass doors from the backyard.

One afternoon, Alyssa and I were unsupervised, which was not unusual. As we ran into the house and flopped down on the old, faded couch in the family room, Alyssa looked at me and said, "I'm hungry."

"Me too," I answered.

She jumped up and skipped over to the kitchen. Holding onto the edge of the kitchen counter for support, she hoisted herself onto the counter and stood up.

I watched from the couch in amazement. I'd never climbed onto our kitchen counter, let alone stood on it. It looked dangerous, but at the same time daring and fun.

I stood up from the couch as Alyssa whisper-yelled at me, "Come on! Come up here with me."

She knew her mother or brothers might come in at any minute

and we needed to act quickly. I slowly walked over to the kitchen and stood next to the counter where she was perched.

At seven years old, she was almost as tall as the cupboards. She looked down at me and said, "Well, come on. Get up here. This is where my mom keeps the sugar and the cookies."

Sweets were definitely my food of choice. Mommy baked lots of cakes and cookies for us, but mostly for daddy. We only got to eat them when she told us we could. In my world, Alyssa was breaking a rule, and I was scared. But as she crouched down and reached for my hand, I felt braver somehow.

"Hold onto the counter and pull yourself up," she told me as she held my hand.

Clumsily, I tried, but I was too uncoordinated. Every time I tried to lift myself up, I didn't know what to do with my feet and I kept falling back down.

Finally, exasperation in her voice, she looked down at me and said, "Just do it! Pull yourself up here. I'm hungry!"

I felt dumb for not being able to lift myself up. But I knew I was smarter than Alyssa because I could read and she couldn't yet. I decided to try one last time to get up on the counter. Using all my strength, I held onto the counter and planted my feet against the bottom cupboards, using them as a springboard for lifting myself up. It worked! At least my torso was now on the counter. I swung my body around and walked my feet up sideways. Sprawled on the counter next to Alyssa, she pointed at me and giggled.

I felt accomplished, as I first got up on my knees, and then stood up next to her, cautiously leaning against the kitchen cupboard behind me.

"Finally!" Alyssa whisper-yelled at me again as she turned and began tiptoeing on the counter to the next row of cupboards.

"The sugar's in this one," she whispered as she motioned for me to follow her.

I was scared. Afraid of getting caught, afraid of falling down, and afraid that Alyssa would be mad at me if I didn't follow her. Clutching on to the cupboard behind me, I inched my way along the counter slowly, careful to not look down.

At last, we reached the other row of cupboards. Alyssa turned back to look at me as she opened the cupboard door. She had to move her feet to the outside edge of the counter to fully open the door. I looked at her, terrified that she might fall.

Reaching into the cupboard, she opened the sugar bowl, stuck her whole hand in, and scooped up as much sugar as she could hold. Tiny white granules fell through her fingers as she stuck her hand into her mouth and licked it clean.

"Do you want some?" she asked as she took her fingers out of her mouth.

Meekly, I looked at her and nodded my head yes.

"Well, you'll have to step around me," she stated firmly. I heard a hint of annoyance in her voice.

Looking down at the counter, where my feet were firmly planted, I was frightened. How could I possibly walk around her on the kitchen counter without falling off? She didn't understand that I was a rule follower who let her daddy touch her even when it felt bad. She didn't understand that I felt helpless and angry.

I looked up at Alyssa. Tears started to well up in my eyes. Quickly, I looked down. I didn't want her to see me crying. Exasperated, she took another handful of sugar and shoved it into her mouth. White crystals fell from her fingers onto the counter next to her small bare feet. After licking each finger clean, she plunged her index finger carefully into the sugar bowl. Sugar granules stuck to her wet finger as she pulled it out and pointed it at me.

"Here," she said, moving closer to me. Her finger was next to my lips. "Open your mouth," she ordered.

Surprised that she wanted me to eat sugar from her finger, I looked at her strangely.

"Just open your mouth. You want some sugar, don't you? We have to hurry up! You don't want my mom to come downstairs and catch us, do you?"

Afraid and hungry, I opened my small mouth and parted my lips as Alyssa gingerly placed her finger between my teeth. Closing my mouth around it, I felt the sugar dissolve on my tongue. It tasted sweet and comforting. I had just broken a rule. I felt powerful.

Without thinking, I quickly jumped off the counter, just like Alyssa. We ran out of the kitchen and up the stairs, anxious to not be seen by her mother. As we walked up the stairs, we heard her brothers laughing in their bedroom. Peeking in, we saw three, or maybe four, teenage boys besides her brothers standing around a record player. Beatles music blared loudly inside the room:

> "...day tripper
> "A one way ticket, yeah
> "It took me so long
> "To find out, and I found out"

Alyssa opened the door and motioned for me to follow her in. Walking behind her, I stood quietly as I entered. The loft room contained a bed situated on the wall where the ceiling slanted down. One window overlooked the front yard. The grayish blue drapes were closed. The record player sat on a rickety brown wooden table. The small forty-five record spun around on the turntable, needle poised on the thin grooves that circled round and round the small disc.

One of the boys closed the door behind me. They all looked at us. Alyssa's brother, Brent, moved toward her. He bent down to whisper in her ear, moving her white blonde hair to one side with his hand. Alyssa giggled as he told her something. Then she looked at me.

Brent stood up and walked back over to the other boys who were standing around the record player. He knew she would play their "singing game," if not just for their attention, at least for something to do. She was the youngest of the family, with three older brothers and one older sister. Definitely an "oops baby," as her sister was seven years older.

Alyssa walked over to where I was standing, just inside the room, next to the closed door. She looked at me coyly. I knew this look. She was going to tell me to do something that we shouldn't. My stomach started to feel nervous. But I was trapped. I couldn't just open the door and leave. She wouldn't like that.

Just as her brother had whispered in her ear, she bent over and softly moved my hair away from my ear. Her fingers felt soft and gentle. Her breath tickled my ear as she told me what the boys wanted us to do. I listened stone-faced. I had heard this request before, just not in this house. I knew how to play this game.

Leaning against me, Alyssa gently nudged me toward the boys who looked at us as if we might be willing to play. Shorts and panties down around our ankles, we were lifted onto the boys' laps by their scrawny teenage hands and arms. As they hoisted us up, and poised us on their crotches, they told us to yell and scream. Wrapping their sweaty hands around our small bellies, as we sat in their laps, they jiggled us up and down and from side to side. Clothed, they manipulated Alyssa and I, our small seven-year-old bodies, as if we were puppets, controlling our movements.

When the song ended, one of the boys, who was watching but not participating, got up and lifted the needle off the record. He looked back at us, nodded, and then carefully placed the needle back on the beginning groove. The music blared again:

"Day tripper, yeah.
One way ticket, yeah."

Footsteps on the stairs signaled the end of the game. Quickly, the boys nudged us off their laps and told us to pull up our pants. I looked over at Alyssa. She had already redressed. I quickly pulled up my white cotton panties and blue shorts. But I didn't want the game to end. I was having fun. We were all yelling and singing and listening to music. It felt special, grown up, and secret, my three well-established feelings. Familiar and comfortable.

Alyssa ran toward the brown bedroom door, turned the door knob, and slipped out. From just beyond the slightly opened door, she turned her head and motioned for me to follow her. Standing next to the boy who'd been holding me on his lap, I glanced up at his face. He looked scared. His mouth closed, his eyes looked straight ahead, toward the record player. His hands lay over the front of his pants. He pushed both palms down on his crotch, squinting his eyes closed and clenching his jaw.

I turned toward the slightly open door and walked out of the room. Alyssa grabbed my hand. It felt slightly damp. We hurried along the hall toward her bedroom. She cautiously pushed open her white bedroom door, and we slipped inside just as we heard her mother's footsteps at the top of the wooden staircase. As her mother's shoes sank into the brown shag carpet that covered the hallway and the upstairs bedrooms, Alyssa and I looked at each other and softly giggled. I smiled. We had a secret. I liked secrets.

SAINT HILL MANOR, EAST GRINSTEAD, WEST SUSSEX, ENGLAND, CIRCA 1966–1967

I n mommy's bedroom closet, hanging neatly side by side, were at least eight different cotton print housedresses, purchased, evidently, for our trip to England. These were not her usual 1960s uniform of black pants and a white cotton blouse.

We took our passport picture at a photography studio in downtown Slidell. Mommy sat on a small stool, wearing a white blouse and make-up, her short brownish-red hair washed, set, combed, and teased up ever so slightly at the top. Bangs hung down over her forehead, framing her blue eyes. Lips closed, no smile, per passport protocol. Just a determined look, as if she was staring directly at L. Ron Hubbard, who continued to promote Scientology, but more grandly than before at Saint Hill Manor.

Standing next to mommy, my unsmiling face looked sadly at the camera. She'd cut my hair the day before the pictures. A pixie bowl cut with one tuft of wispy bangs that she'd missed, accidentally, I guess, hung down on my forehead. I wore a navy blue dress, but it looked black in the picture.

My little brother sat next to me. His blonde cowlick stood up on end at the top of his head, and his upper lip sported a new cold sore. Mommy had dragged him out of his Superman pajamas and made him begrudgingly put on a striped and collared cotton shirt. He looked forlorn.

The three of us, one unit, one photograph, getting ready to fly across the Atlantic Ocean to England. To Scientology's new headquarters. Perhaps feeling hopeful, mommy had bought new dresses, thinking that might make her excited to leave Slidell, and 1960s suburbia, to reenter the world of Scientology. A way of living she seemed to have temporarily escaped.

Momentarily, it seemed that Southern suburbia had replaced Scientology's hold on both my parents. But Sunday brunches in New Orleans, playing cards with the next-door neighbors, and trying out new Betty Crocker recipes couldn't quite stand up to "Clearing the planet" and taking the next Scientology course to attain "Total Freedom."

The plan to go to Saint Hill started with daddy. He'd just read *The Auditor*, a Scientology newspaper that came in the mail to our house, often. Sometimes I'd pick it up and look at the pictures, which were mostly of L. Ron Hubbard, Saint Hill Manor, and Scientologists I didn't know. But I didn't read much of it. The articles were long and looked boring. They were usually about becoming Clear, or different kinds of auditing and processing. There were also lists of names of Scientologists who had completed trainings or who were now "Clear."

I really wasn't sure what most of the articles were talking about, but I definitely knew about the word "Clear." I'd heard daddy tell mommy the definition many times. I also knew that daddy had a Clear Bracelet and mommy didn't.

Every night, usually after dinner, daddy looked through the mail. Whenever *The Auditor* came, daddy seemed excited. He loved reading it out loud to mommy as she sat at the kitchen table with her cigarettes and ashtray, listening to the latest Scientology news and information.

This particular issue of *The Auditor* was printed in green ink with large bold headings that read, "Get Processed in 1966, Get Released in 1966, Get Trained in 1966." As daddy read each section aloud, his voice got louder and he sounded more and more excited.

I watched mommy's face. At first, she smiled and commented while daddy read the names of the current "Clears" and "Releases."

"Oh, yes, I remember her from D.C. Where's she living now?" mommy asked.

Suddenly, daddy jumped out of his chair and started walking around the kitchen and family room as he told mommy, "Gloria, listen to this, Ron says that by the end of 1966, Saint Hill will have expanded to 266 staff members, and occupy twice the space. And staff members get free Power Processing and training at half the professional rate. Gloria, we've got to go!"

When daddy finished, mommy stopped smiling and told him, in a serious voice, "Paul, we can't go to Saint Hill. I can't take Pammy out of school until June."

The words were barely out of mommy's mouth when the explosion happened.

"What do you mean we can't go to Saint Hill?!" Shaking the newspaper at her, he continued to bellow, "Listen, I've been biding my time here in Slidell, working my ass off to buy all this fancy new furniture."

Daddy wagged his finger toward the living room, where all the new furniture lived.

Then he pointed his finger at mommy as he yelled, "We sure as hell CAN go to Saint Hill! We can even work there!"

Mommy stood up and walked toward daddy. Gently, she touched his arm and pleaded, "Paul, we can't go now. I promise, we'll go, but not yet."

Still touching his arm, she continued, "Anyway, we can't afford it. The Briefing Course costs a thousand dollars, each. Plane flights and housing will cost even more."

"Look at the prices," she added as she pointed to the page that daddy held in his hand.

Mommy ended her plea by touching daddy on the arm again as she told him, "Paul, we just don't have that kind of money."

Daddy jerked his arm away from mommy and stomped out of the room. A few minutes later, I heard the stereo blasting. It was daddy's favorite song by Herb Alpert & the Tijuana Brass. I knew it well.

• • •

We left in the summer of 1967, on a double-decker Delta flight across the Atlantic. Mommy looked happy as she took us up to the second deck of the plane and ordered a cocktail. Looking out at the night sky, it was dark and cloudless. My little brother and I drank 7 Up with ice out of small plastic cups. It felt like we were on an adventure!

It was a long cab ride from the London airport to the small town of Tunbridge Wells and the Harewood Hotel, which offered a small room with one bed, a hot plate, and a tiny English fridge. Mommy opened the hotel room door, and surveyed the contents of the room. She looked sad and tired. Picking up the hotel phone, which sat on a small table near the small bed, she told the operator she wanted to make a call to the United States.

With a little assistance, she called daddy. He hadn't traveled with us. In the end, my parents must have decided that daddy would stay in Slidell and keep working until he could join us. Their hushed phone conversation was tense, but firm. This wasn't what they'd agreed upon.

The hotel and the room would not work. There was no kitchen to cook in, as promised, and the hot plate and small fridge would not suffice. Also, there was only one bed, and it was too small to comfortably fit the three of us. Mommy told daddy that he needed to do something, and he needed to do it immediately.

Somehow, the next day, we ended up in a very large room, probably a suite by Harewood Hotel standards. We had two bedrooms and one bathroom, along with a view of the gardens, or the trees and bushes that they referred to as the gardens. There was a metal jungle gym nestled in the middle, surrounded by foliage. Sometimes, but not often, my little brother and I were allowed to go outside and climb on it unsupervised.

Our first night there, we settled in and went to the dining room for dinner. Mommy, my little brother, and I sat at a large dining table opposite other Scientology guests of the hotel. We were quiet and reserved children, perfect by English standards. The first course, fish, came out served on a platter. Fully intact, eyes and all, several fish lay there ready to be neatly cut, forked, and eaten through their shiny translucent scales, heads and tails cushioned on a pillow of lettuce.

After taking one look at this entree, knowing full well we weren't going to eat it, mommy ordered us trifle, basically dessert for dinner! We looked at her incredulously as the gooey sponge cake laden with berries and sweet creamy custard arrived at our table. Lifting our spoons, we plunged through the cream to the berries and jam cushioned between the yellow cake. My little brother and I stole silent sideways glances at each other as we happily ate the delicious English treat.

Not bad, I thought, as we plotted and planned our next meal. Fairly quickly, we both convinced mommy that we'd only eat dessert for dinner. Amazingly, she consented to our request, and English trifle was sent to our hotel room nightly.

While mommy went out to dinner, socializing with the Scientologists she'd met at the hotel and at Saint Hill, my little brother and I dug into our treat with our silver spoons. We'd both learned early on in our relatively young lives, from both of our parents, but mostly from mommy, the chief enabler, how to stuff down our feelings, especially with food.

After devouring the trifle each evening, we topped off our sweet feast with cups of English tea, poured from a silver teapot into our waiting teacups. Liberal splashes of cream and four cubes of sugar dropped into our lukewarm tea water created the sugary sleep-inducing beverage we both craved, and learned to depend on, before going to bed. We also enjoyed munching on English biscuits, basically cookies, throughout the evening. Lacking adult supervision, holed up in a hotel room, we devised our own eating schedule.

• • •

In September, mommy enrolled us in a local English Episcopal church school that my little brother and I briefly attended. Uniforms were required. Mine was a white button-down oxford collared blouse and a gray pleated skirt. For physical education, we just changed our shoes. After the first week of school, the headmistress informed mommy that I needed plimsolls, a black English tennis shoe, somewhat like Keds. I needed them for athletics, which was basically P.E. class.

However, mommy could not for the life of her locate the necessary plimsolls. Each day that I didn't have them, I cringed, knowing that the nice English church school teacher would sternly tell me how they were required, and then look at me with pity and confusion.

I'm sure she thought, why can't her American mother buy this poor child these shoes? And, sadly, we've lent her a pair, but poor thing, they're too big and her feet somewhat flip around in the toe, no matter how tight we help her tie the laces.

Throughout the entire month or so that we attended the school, my uncoordinated nine-year-old body ran, jumped rope, and hit whiffle balls wearing the plimsoll loaners. Too busy listening to L. Ron Hubbard's lectures at Saint Hill, mommy became an absent and uninvolved parent.

While living and working at Saint Hill, L. Ron Hubbard gave many lectures, which were all recorded. Mommy was required, along with the many other Scientologists who traveled to Saint Hill, to listen to these taped recordings of his lectures as part of her daily training. Winding and rewinding the tape recorder to hear Hubbard's every word as he espoused Scientology truths, she was also required to take copious notes.

But from my vantage point, mommy appeared to be happy at Saint Hill. Although she was away from daddy, in a foreign country, with few friends and only fellow Scientologists to socialize with, she appeared more at ease, as if she was free to be herself.

Her smiles even seemed less tense. Listening to her conversations with Scientologists at the hotel, I overheard her tell them how she loved the beauty of the green hills that surrounded Saint Hill in the West Sussex countryside. Adding that it reminded her, just a little, of Kansas, where she'd grown up.

But while mommy studied at Saint Hill, my little brother and I spent our afternoons in an English garden thick with gooseberries, blackberries, and raspberries. Hydrangeas grew in huge bushes along the back of the two-story house with a red door.

Inside, the radio played:

"Would you like to fly in my beautiful balloon.
We can sail the skies together, you and I.
Up, up and away. In my beautiful, my beautiful balloon."

Outside, Maggie, model-thin, beautiful, dark-haired babysitter lay on a rickety chaise lounge covered with a thin red-and-white-striped towel. Sunglasses covered her sea-blue eyes, fringed with jet black lashes. While her baby, about nine months old, napped peacefully in her wooden crib, just up the five steps to the screened back door and her tiny bedroom, Maggie let us—my little brother, a South African Scientology boy, and me—run free.

Until that day, I'd never tasted anything as exquisite as a fresh berry plucked straight from its twisty vine. The delight was not just the burst of juice in my mouth, but the pure decadence that surrounded the joy of running barefoot in the garden. Freedom! No adult telling us not to run. No reprimands for being too noisy or full of glee.

We ran up and down the berry vines, sunshine streaming through the least thick spots where gooseberries glimmered like shiny alien orbs. They were substantial in size, firm, yet ripe. With my nine-year-old fingers, I picked one, put it to my lips, and popped it into my mouth. I didn't know what to expect. Juicy! A little like a green grape, but sweeter and with tiny seeds. I giggled.

Maggie's care for us was simple. She didn't have to mother us, nor did she want to. We were temporary visitors. Short-term responsibilities. The boys kept busy roughhousing and playing with cars in the playroom. They were noisy, but not bothersome. I was quiet and possibly a bit helpful.

At suppertime, early dinnertime for children in England, Maggie would feed us alongside her sweet cherub-faced baby, who sat in her wooden high chair next to me, my brother, and the South African boy. Her baby would suck on spaghetti covered in pale red sauce, her face a sweet, smiling mess.

Her chubby little fingers grasped the slippery noodles and shoved them into her tiny mouth. We watched in amusement as she ate what we called "red worms." Our childish joke. I think the boys thought of it and laughed aloud at their silliness while Maggie just ignored them.

After supper, Maggie washed up the dishes in the small yellow kitchen with the tiniest little fridge, like a doll's kitchen. I helped by watching the baby. I would stand next to her high chair as she cooed and giggled at me. Sometimes, if I stood close enough to her chair, she'd reach out with her tiny soft fingers and touch my face.

Her little hand moved across my freckled nose to my cheek. When I closed my eyes, her soft baby fingers stroked my blond little-girl lashes and tickled my eyes. I loved her touch. I loved her baby sounds and her sweet innocent smile. With my eyes closed, I dreamily thought, I don't want mommy to come and take us back to the hotel. I want to live with Maggie, her husband Malcolm, and their precious baby. We could be a family.

Away from daddy, an ocean and a continent dividing us, I didn't miss him, his touch, or his smell. He was far away in America. I felt a sense of freedom at Maggie's house that I'd never experienced before. She didn't expect much of us, just that we played, ate our meals, and didn't cause her much trouble. It wasn't hard. Maggie allowed us to be kids. She didn't treat us like small adults.

When mommy came to pick us up after her full day of training at Saint Hill, I felt sad to leave. The Harewood Hotel was stuffy, full of adults, and boring. But we wouldn't be there long. Our next Scientology adventure was right around the corner.

⤜⤛

THE *ROYAL SCOTMAN*'S MAIDEN VOYAGE, SOUTHAMPTON, ENGLAND, NOVEMBER 28, 1967

I t was late in the evening when we left the Harewood Hotel. My little brother and I were told not to change our clothes after school because we were going "somewhere."

When I asked mommy where we were going, she remained secretive and replied, "It's somewhere far. We have to drive at night to get there."

Although I was curious, I'd learned not to ask too many questions.

Mommy's olive green trunk had already been packed with all our clothes and belongings. The trunk reminded me of something my little brother's G.I. Joe dolls might have used, but in miniature form, complete with attached dog tags. I'm not sure why she packed a trunk and not a suitcase. Perhaps a trunk would better transport our belongings onto the ship.

We drove in the dark. I dozed on and off during the long drive. When I awoke, I looked out the back car window and saw the outline of the hull of a large ship against the cloudy night sky. We'd arrived at the docks in Southampton. The driver of the car, maybe a fellow Scientologist, or a crew member from the *Royal Scotman*, stopped the car, turned off the engine, and told mommy we needed to board quickly and quietly. He seemed impatient and nervous.

I'd never been to a dock, or anywhere near the sea. The ship looked huge! Black and ominous, silhouetted by the headlights of the car. Mommy and the man got out of the car first. Then mommy opened the back car door for me and my little brother, who'd fallen asleep. I nudged him with my elbow and woke him up.

Sleepy, and unsure of where we were, he asked me, "Who's that?" and pointed to the man.

I shrugged and replied in a loud whisper, "Come on. We're here!"

The man led us to the end of a gangplank that rested on the concrete dock. As I looked up the stairs from the dock, he told us again that we needed to be very quiet. He was probably afraid we were noisy kids. Mommy held my little brother's hand and I followed behind her. It was dark. I held on tightly to the metal handrail.

When we reached the top, we stepped off the metal stairs and onto the wooden deck of the ship. It was too dark to see much, but I could make out a few shadowy figures on the top deck. The man led us to an opening where more metal stairs descended into the hull of the ship. Carefully, he led the three of us down the dark steps, which smelled like wet playground equipment after it rains.

It was cold inside the ship. I shivered as we walked down a long corridor. It seemed like a very long walk, especially because I couldn't see where we were going. Finally, the man stopped and motioned for mommy to enter a dark room that was framed by a metal doorway. As we followed behind her, I saw shadowy rows of bunk beds with small mounds covered by blankets.

Mommy placed my little brother onto an empty bottom bunk, and then helped me climb onto the top bunk above him. Still wearing my gray pleated uniform skirt and white cotton blouse, she covered me with one of the thin blankets. It felt itchy and rough against my arms and legs. She told me to go to sleep as she pulled the covers around me. Then she left.

I'm not sure how long I lay there before I fell asleep. In the darkness, I tried to make out the shapes of the other beds, to see if anyone else was in the room with us, but I couldn't. Although mommy was gone, I don't remember feeling scared. Maybe because I'd become used to her leaving my little brother and me alone at the hotel. Feeling more curious than anything else, I wondered what it was going to be like living on this ship.

The *Royal Scotman* set sail from Southampton, England, into dark and stormy waters with an inexperienced crew of young and fearless Scientologists. Throughout the night, the ship lurched, rocking and rolling in the high seas until she miraculously made her way into calmer waters in the Mediterranean Sea.

Hana Eltringham, a former Scientologist and crew member recounted the hair-raising maiden voyage:

> *"We sailed out of the Channel that evening into an awful storm. The engine room was in a very bad condition; the main engines were not running very well and neither were the generators and because the paint was so dirty in the engine room you couldn't follow which were the water lines and which were the fuel lines. Halfway*

*between Southampton and Brest, one of the generators conked out.
I was on bridge watch as officer of the deck. We were between three
to five miles off the northwest tip of France and I could see ahead,
on the port side, the buoys marking the rocky coastline going south.
But as we came around to try and get into the estuary toward Brest,
I noticed that the red-flashing buoys were swinging across the bow of
the ship, and I realized we were caught in a riptide and were being
pushed toward the rocks. The ship started to wallow very badly
and each time she went over she took longer to recover. Although
she had stabilizers, she went from a five degree roll to almost a
twenty-five degree roll and on the last roll to port she staggered.
We were all hanging on to the bridge and at that moment the old
man [Hubbard] began screaming at Bill Robertson, the navigator,
'Get us on a course out of here! Get us on a course out of here!' He
was really bellowing. The ship started to stagger around, very slowly
and painfully. It was scary. I was terrified and I think LRH was
too, the way he was screaming and holding on to the bridge and
glaring at us."*

Thankfully, my little brother and I slept through much of the
storm. I woke up once to the sound of the ship creaking. Lying in
bed, I could hear loud banging noises. But never having been on a
ship before, I didn't know that the sounds I heard and the movement
I felt were due to the storm.

Early the next morning, after eating breakfast in the dining area,
mommy came and got us. She told us we were going to the top deck
of the ship to help clean up from the storm. The deck was still wet
from the rain, and the waves that had crashed over the bow the night
before. As we walked up the metal stairs, I held onto the handrail

to steady myself. The white paint that covered it was peeling off, revealing rusty, red corroded metal underneath.

As soon as my little brother and I stepped onto the deck, we saw quite a few people who were wiping down the wet railings and mopping up water that had washed onto the deck. Mommy took my little brother and I over to a brass bell that was partially exposed, but mostly surrounded by a metal enclosure. I wasn't sure what the bell was used for, but mommy quickly told my little brother to start polishing it. Grasping a tattered white rag that she'd placed in his small hand, he gingerly rubbed the cloth over the top of the bell.

Mommy stood over him commenting on his efforts, "Wow! That bell looks great! You're really making it shine!"

Her praise seemed deliberate and loud, like she was shouting so everyone around us could hear. My little brother looked up at her sadly and let the rag fall on the damp deck.

Mommy bent down and spoke to him in an urgent, but hushed voice, "You need to keep shining the bell. HE is walking around the deck. I want HIM to see what a good job you're doing."

Looking pleadingly at mommy, my little brother whimpered, "I don't want to shine it. I'm cold. I want to go inside."

As he spoke, his little lips shivered and his short light brown hair was blown and tousled by the crisp sea breeze. Just then, LRH—as he was often referred to by the Scientologists on the ship—began walking toward them. Dressed all in white with a blue ascot tie around his neck and a white captain's hat covering his head, he surveyed the activity on the deck, nodding to individuals who were busy mopping, polishing, and generally looking busy in order to please him. I'd moved away from mommy and my little brother.

Standing next to the chipped white railing on the side of the ship, holding my little brother's dirty white rag in my hand, I moved it across the railing, catching it on the rusted spots where the paint had peeled off.

Out of the corner of my eye I saw L. Ron Hubbard move toward me. Intently, I looked down and moved my rag more vigorously, hoping for a compliment. But as he approached the railing, he looked directly over me at the sea and the waves on the horizon, never once acknowledging my presence. I was of no importance to him, as if I was invisible.

However, what was important to Hubbard, was that approximately four months prior to the maiden voyage of the *Royal Scotman*, Scientology's tax-exempt status had been revoked by the Internal Revenue Service. The U.S. Court of Claims in Washington, D.C., ruled on the IRS contention that the founding church in D.C., was not a church, but a profit-making, commercial enterprise.

In its decision, the Court wrote, *"What emerges from these facts is the inference that the Hubbard family was entitled to make ready, personal use of the corporate earnings."*

While on the ship, in a calculated response to this ruling, Hubbard announced his resignation as president of the Church of Scientology by explaining that the Church was sufficiently well-established to survive without his leadership.

But as I witnessed, as a young child, it was clear that Hubbard, who was sailing the Mediterranean Sea tax-free, and masquerading as a "writer in seclusion," was still very much in charge.

SHIP LIFE

We stood in our underwear, shirtless and bare-chested. The water stung as it hit my skin. I closed my eyes, but didn't yell. What good would screaming do anyway? We were kids. We did what we were told. The adults were in charge.

At least we were told that repeatedly, along with phrases like, "Don't make Ron mad." Or, "LRH wants this done now!"

We were being hosed down by the crazy nanny in the metal bathroom stalls of the ship.

She aimed the water hose at us and yelled, "It's time to clean you kids up!"

My little brother hid behind me while the other children, ranging in age from about four years old to probably twelve years old covered their faces or turned around so only their backs were stung by the spray of water. The hose was large and thick. It reminded me of a fire truck hose, made of stiff fabric with a brass-colored nozzle.

After being hosed down, my little brother and I, along with the other kids, walked out of the dark and unventilated bathroom that housed sinks, showers and toilets. We were marched down the dark corridors of the inner, bowels of the ship to our berths.

The nanny then directed us to quickly get dressed, "Let's go kids! I'm not waiting for any of you."

Each of us pulled out clothes from a duffel bag next to our bunks as we shoved our wet undershirts and underwear into the same bag. I don't remember who did our laundry, but we did learn to dress and undress quickly, most likely wearing the same dirty clothing multiple days in a row.

The nursery, or kids' berth, was similar to our dormitory style-room on the ship, except for the makeshift baby paraphernalia that was haphazardly placed there, like the high chair fashioned out of a metal table and chairs, and the playpen which resembled a mesh dirty-clothes hamper.

The baby we watched was probably about seven or eight months old, give or take a month or two. Being a kid myself, it was hard to gauge the age of babies. The baby didn't walk yet, but she could pull herself up on the side of her mesh cage. She was sweet and easy to take care of, which seemed to be the job of the other young girl in the nursery, who was probably only a year older than I was. The nanny let her do most of the babysitting chores, but sometimes I was allowed to help.

Taking care of the baby was like having a live doll that we got to play with every day. We fed her, changed her diaper, and put her to sleep. I loved spending time with the baby! But the girl who'd been tasked with taking care of her rarely smiled. She seemed almost robotic when she performed the daily chore of feeding the baby.

Opening the jar of baby food, lifting the spoon, dipping it in the yellow, orange, or green mush and then putting the spoon into the baby's mouth. She knew just how to pull the spoon out and cleanly wipe the corners of the baby's lips so there weren't any messy remnants that needed to be wiped off the baby's face. I watched in awe. I'd never fed a real baby before, and I felt very intimidated by the girl's precision, and by what I considered to be her perfect baby feeding skills.

One day, while I watched the feeding routine, I asked her if I could feed the baby. The girl looked at me blankly. She had thin, long blonde hair parted perfectly right down the middle of her head. It hung straight down the sides of her thin face. Her eyes were big and blue, yet devoid of expression.

She looked at me, and said in a serious tone, "Yes, you can try," as she handed me the spoon and extended her arm out for me to take the open jar of food.

It smelled like bananas. I held the jar in my left hand and dipped the spoon inside to retrieve a dollop of the yellow goo. As I lifted the spoon and looked at the sweet little baby standing in her playpen, I felt grown-up, capable, important, and, above all else, needed.

• • •

One night, our dinner menu took an unusual turn. Brownish

pieces of meat on white plates were passed down a gray metal staircase by adults to the room below. We'd been told to stay there and wait. There were no tables, chairs, or bathroom facilities. A little boy who needed to pee did so, pulling his pants down to his ankles, and aimed at a corner of the room.

At first curious, and then bewildered, I watched his small bare bottom and the steady stream of yellow urine as it hit the floor, and then trickled slowly into the corner of the room. No adults were present to reprimand him.

As the plates continued to be passed down the staircase, I heard one of the other children ask the man at the top of the stairs, "What's this?"

The man with dark brownish eyes and a wide smile replied, "It's tongue. A little salty, but edible."

My mind reeled. What? Whose tongue? I looked closer at the brownish slab I'd been handed and noticed the whitish dots that covered the top of the meat. The smell of fresh urine and salt filled the room. I felt sick.

I heard a few of the other kids say, "Yuck! I'm not eating a tongue!"

Me neither, I thought. Disgusting! Although I could hear my stomach rumbling, I decided not to take a dinner plate.

In the meantime, the belligerent boys, who each held a white plate with the brownish substance balanced in the center, started passing their plates back up the stairs to the man crouched at the top.

As the man looked down at us, he shrugged and said, "Suit yourself," taking each untouched slab and plate from the boys and handing them to another adult, whose black shoes and pants were all that was visible from the room below. We remained hungry, which became a familiar feeling while on the ship.

Not surprisingly, provisions that were purchased at the last port had been depleted, eaten, and consumed. Tongue must have been the only option, as the *Royal Scotman* had been unable to find a friendly port to restock provisions, as documented by former crew members:

> *"Denied entry into Gibraltar, the* Royal Scotman *continued into the Mediterranean under her emergency steering and set a course for the little principality of Monaco, where Hubbard hoped he would be more welcome. Food and water were running low and the cook was reduced to serving soup made with seawater by the time the ship approached Monte Carlo in early December. She was too big to enter the harbor, but the port authorities agreed to her being refueled and reprovisioned by lighters, and engineers were brought on board to repair the steering. From Monaco, the* Royal Scotman *sailed to Cagliari in Sardinia, where she docked for the first time since leaving Southampton."*

A few ports later, while docked in Valencia, Spain, my little brother and I went off the ship with mommy to a restaurant close to where the *Royal Scotman* was anchored. I'm not sure why she was allowed to take us off the ship, or if other Scientologists were with us.

While mommy, my little brother, and I ate spaghetti, the waiter brought us a basket of bread. Mommy asked him for some butter, but in English. The Spanish waiter didn't speak or understand English, so mommy used hand gestures and pretended to butter a piece of bread. Finally, the waiter exclaimed, "Ah! Mantequilla."

Mommy seemed very happy when he returned to our table with an extra basket of bread and several plates of butter. That was one of the best meals we ate.

While living onboard the ship, perhaps due to my parents' earlier connection with Mary Sue and L. Ron Hubbard, my little brother and I were tutored alongside the Hubbard children. The one exception was Hubbard's oldest daughter, sixteen-year-old Diana, who was heavily immersed in Scientology and other responsibilities, as dictated by her father.

Our poor tutor was a Scientologist named Sylvia Hare, who was charged with educating us. She was probably in her late forties or early fifties, quite old compared to the average age on the ship.

A notice to all crew and Scientologists onboard was posted in the main dining areas on the ship, which explained how the Hubbard children, as well as me, my little brother, and the other handful of children onboard, were to be treated:

> "A tutor will be provided for the children, who will be assigned regular hours of work and play. Anyone who deprives a child of his or her work or play will be assigned to a condition of nonexistence. (Non-existence: Must wear old clothes. May not bathe. Women must not wear make-up or have hairdo's. Men may not shave. No lunch hour....)"

Mary Sue Hubbard made sure that her children were seen as a priority on the ship. Afterall, this was their new home. Saint Hill and their idyllic lifestyle in the English countryside had been usurped, and she was tasked with recreating their familial routines in a new, perhaps somewhat less than desirable setting.

As we gathered in our own private study, I watched Arthur, who was closest to my age. He liked to draw. Suzette, his sister, who was a bit older, sat on the ledge of the windows, just above the top of the seats. She hung her long legs over the edge, perched against the burgundy velvet curtains that were pulled closed.

Suzette's thick red hair bobbed and bounced on her head as she jumped from seat to ledge and back again. Her freckled face and impish grin reminded me of Peter Pan. It seemed as if she could start flying around the room at any time.

Collectively, we were an interesting yet disinterested group of students. But I did love reading about the Seven Wonders of the Ancient World from *World Book Encyclopedias* that were somehow part of our curriculum. We also learned a few silly songs that we performed for LRH and the crew one night. Other than that, I'm not sure much learning occurred.

Quentin, L. Ron Hubbard's older son, was as the British might have called him, a "dapper young chap." Dressed all in white, literally, from the white brimmed seaman's cap he wore over his sandy-blonde, longish hair, to the white patent leather boots he wore on his feet, he was the epitome of cleanliness. At thirteen years old, he was slightly prepubescent, betwixt and between, yet still childish in his demeanor. He was not at all a sullen preteen.

Sweet by nature, he gladly showed me his private quarters on the ship one afternoon. As we walked together down the long inner corridor to his room, from our tutoring quarters at the end of the ship, I felt excited and important. It was the first time that another child on the ship, even though he was older, wanted to spend time with me, talk to me, and acknowledge my existence.

His small cabin included his own bed, desk, dreser, closet, and bathroom. It was beautiful, at least to my nine-year-old eyes. The walls were a deep, rich, polished smooth wood. His bottom bunk was meticulously made, corners tucked under, military-style. It was impeccably neat. He took such pride in his tidiness and his personal space.

While I stood silently, admiring Quentin's room, he turned and asked me, "Now, Pam, don't you have a cabin like this? On the lower deck?"

When I shook my head that I didn't, he promptly replied, "Well, you definitely should. I'll speak to Mummy about that."

I'm pretty sure that he never did speak to Mary Sue about it. Or if he tried to question my accommodations that he was met with anything more than a sideways glance that conveyed, "Really none of your business, dear. Now, run along."

After briefly touring his cabin, we walked outside and stood on the wooden deck with the white metal railing. We were docked, and from this side of the ship, we had a view of the port below, which housed pallets of boxes. Trucks could be seen driving by and several groups of men were walking and working at the dock. As we stood at the railing watching the men move about, Quentin and I talked. Actually, Quentin did most of the talking. I just listened.

He was excited, animated, and full of wonder. He chattered away about seeing the world. But as he looked out over the dock and the workers, I don't believe he really saw them. He was either looking past them, or through them, as if he wore special glasses that could see beyond the reality in which he existed and lived.

He talked about what he might do when he was off the ship. Travel, fly an airplane, and how we might meet each other again one day. I looked at him intently. He was so full of life and so sweet. I was a painfully shy little girl from Slidell, Louisiana, plucked from my Southern suburban life and thrown into an unknown world. We were truly strangers.

Sadly, years later at the young age of twenty-two, Quentin allegedly took his own life. According to those who knew Quentin, he'd tried hard to measure up to his father's expectations, but all he wanted was to leave Scientology to fly airplanes.

It was also suspected that Quentin was a homosexual, which infuriated his father, L. Ron Hubbard, who was purported to be homophobic. His immediate response to his son's death was anger and rage that Quentin had let him down, followed by both an internal and public cover-up of his son's death and the circumstances surrounding his alleged suicide.

Arthur was my age. Nine years old. Actually, a few months older. I was born after him, although Mary Sue and mommy were pregnant at the same time in Washington, D.C., Arthur was her fourth and last child, the end of the line.

Although Arthur and I were very close in age, we had very little to say to each other. He seemed totally absorbed in his drawings and not the least bit interested in me. He was the baby of the family, and Suzette kept an older, sisterly eye on him, while Quentin seemed to ignore him.

Aboard their new home, the Hubbard children had free rein to wander as they liked and to behave as they chose, while my little brother and I, along with the other children onboard, were watched closely, and expected to follow the orders of our Scientology nanny.

ETHICS &
THE SEA ORGANIZATION

We didn't see or spend much time at all with mommy while she was sequestered elsewhere on the ship, receiving auditing from a Scientologist named Scott Leland, since deceased.

While working on "her case," mommy wasn't allowed to visit us, or to have much contact with anyone, aside from her auditor and other personnel who controlled the auditing environment. Ethics was applied to anyone who deviated from the stringent rules that were imposed.

According to Scientology literature:

> *"The group itself brings pressure to bear to secure conformity, in part because being associated with someone whose Ethics are suspect may lead to suspicion about their own. It is a truly illuminating experience to be assigned a Condition of Liability... Colleagues whom you regarded as friends seem suddenly distant. They won't talk to you.*

They don't offer you cigarettes or suggest you take a swig out of their Coke bottle. In some really Eager Beaver cases, they even refuse your cigarettes when you offer them!"

On the ship, a Condition of Liability was like having to wear a "Scarlet Letter." If you were deemed to be guilty of this Condition, you wore a white rag tied around your upper arm, clearly displayed for all to see. You were also assigned various menial tasks, like cleaning toilets and scraping rust off the metal railings of the ship.

I'm not sure if mommy was ever assigned a Condition of Liability for trying to see us, or for some other infraction, but she was very nervous anytime she stopped by the nursery to say hello to me and my little brother. She'd just walk by and wave, or give my little brother a quick hug, and then immediately leave, as if she was being followed.

Any Ethical actions or codes that she might have been assigned, or made to endure, were part of life on the ship. Scientology's Code of Ethics stated:

"The recruit begins applying the Ethics codes to himself rather than waiting to have them applied to him by the Ethics Officer. Henceforth should he suffer any nagging skepticism he will realize that it is not a rational response but simply the consequence of his being in a 'Condition of Doubt.' Having assigned himself to this Condition, he can then proceed to apply the Ethics formula and begin to work his way out. The individual begins to conceive of the system of social control as central to the survival of the movement, hence Ethics sanctions are not merely something to submit to and suffer, they are to be welcomed as a source of enlightenment."

While on the *Royal Scotman*, mommy wrote about her "Ethical Treatment" after reaching the state of "Clear:"

> *"I have just completed three days of fabulous wins with Ethics. I really know what Ethics is all about now. Previously I'd had it confused with punishment, which it's not at all. Clarice has helped me to make my environment safer so that now I can be audited successfully. I really know what it means to be 'salvaged with Ethics' and it's great!"*
> **Gloria Nickel, Clear No. 700**

> *"So, this is Ethics! It's beautiful. It's safe and helpful. I can really see for once how it makes things right so tech can go in."*
> **Gloria Nickel, Clear No. 700**

It's hard to imagine what she might have meant to be "salvaged with Ethics," unless she meant she was away from her family, and especially daddy.

But years later, when mommy shared stories of life on the *Royal Scotman*, any Conditions of Liability or Ethics sanctions she experienced were never part of her repertoire. Instead, in her version, she spoke as if she'd taken a bit of a European mini-cruise to a few countries where she saw interesting sights and met locals who were kind and helpful. Perhaps her "reimagined" stories provided her with a way to replace the insanity she experienced with some degree of perceived normalcy.

• • •

Just a few months after setting sail, while docked in Valencia, Spain, we were boarded off the ship, along with all the other Scientologists who were not Sea Org members.

By January of 1968, the Sea Organization, or Sea Org as it was called, was in full swing onboard the *Royal Scotman*, and "civilians" were being sent off the ship. The choice to join the Sea Org and stay on the ship or to leave had thankfully been made for mommy. Women with small children in hand were not part of Hubbard's new plan.

Sea Org recruits were, and still are, required to sign a billion-year contract. Not surprisingly, most do sign on with the intention of serving the full length of their contract, mainly because they believe themselves to be thetans, or infinite beings.

According to L. Ron Hubbard, thetans are defined as: "*having no mass, no wavelength, no energy, no measurable qualities, and no time or location in space except by consideration or postulate. The spirit is not a thing. It is the creator of things.*"

Scientologists, as predicated by L. Ron Hubbard, also believe that they, as thetans, will never die, but instead "drop and pick up meat bodies" to continue their tireless work of "Clearing the planet" and ultimately the entire universe. Even if mommy could have joined the Sea Org, I don't believe she was ready to agree to an immortality that demanded such a steep commitment.

As we waited to be sent back to the U.S., the three of us sat at a small metal table on the outside patio of a restaurant located next to the dock. In the center of the table was a glass container filled with sugar. It was the kind that the sugar easily pours out of, with a silver metal lid at the top, that opens as you turn the container over.

Hungry and bored, my little brother and I decided, somewhat boldly, to pick up the container and pour the white sugar over the slices of bread that mommy had buttered for us. As I took a bite of the bread, sweet and sugary, I watched mommy out of the corner of my eye. She had NEVER let us do this before! I waited to see what she'd say or do.

Sitting across from me, but next to my little brother, mommy gazed off into the distance. It was a warm morning, with a light ocean breeze that smelled like salt and sea mixed together. It felt good to be outside.

My little brother and I quickly ate our slices of bread. While on the ship, we had learned that our next meal might not be as tasty. As we took bites, some of the sugar spilled off onto the metal tabletop. Mommy looked down at the spilled sugar, and then looked back up at my little brother and me. But I could tell by the way she looked at us, that she didn't really see us. She was elsewhere.

Without saying a word, she pulled a long, thin cigarette from its box. I read the brand, KOOL, written on the turquoise blue and green menthol cigarette package. The cellophane wrapper was still intact, except at the top, at the silver-colored line, where she'd opened it. Mommy lit the cigarette with a match and inhaled deeply. I watched, intently, as she performed her soothing ritual. I hadn't seen her smoke for quite a while, not that she hadn't, but because we weren't together on the ship.

I wasn't sure if I'd missed her, or if she'd missed me. We sat in silence, choosing not to speak of our time on the ship or what might happen next. Eating slices of buttered bread, spilling sugar on the table between bites, my little brother and I were happy to be eating something sweet and comforting, and to be off the ship.

As mommy continued smoking, her long, slender fingers carefully held her cigarette. Putting it to her mouth, she pursed her lips around the white filtered tip, inhaled deeply, and then puffed out the smoke in one large exhale, just as I remembered. We sat there for a very long time, all three at peace in our denial and our preferred addictions. Our journey had been brief, but memorable.

BACK HOME, CIRCA 1968

I don't really remember the flight home or our reunion with daddy. Surprisingly, he never joined us in England or on the ship. Had he planned to? I don't know. Did I miss him? I'm not sure.

Once we were back in Louisiana, life returned to normal for my little brother and I as we went back to school. Fourth grade seemed easy enough for me, but listening to my parents argue and fight was not.

My little brother and I hid behind the turquoise faux leather couch in the family room. The TV was on, but we weren't watching it, mesmerized instead by the scene unfolding in our kitchen and family room. As we crouched down behind the couch, I peered around the arm of vinyl. Seated at the kitchen table, cigarette in hand, eyes wild with rage, an empty cup of coffee teetered in mommy's other hand.

"You bastard!" she yelled. "Get that shit-eating grin off your face!"

But daddy just continued to grin and stare at her, with a crazy look in his eyes, as the coffee she'd just thrown at him slowly dripped from his forehead to his nose, and onto the Formica tabletop, forming a tiny light-brown pool of liquid.

"Where the hell do you think I should go?" she demanded. "I'm not going back to Saint Hill!" she bellowed at him.

Mommy stood up and walked to the kitchen. I shrank down to make myself as small as possible, terrified that she was going to see us. But nothing could deter her from her rant. I knew this about mommy. I could predict her words, her actions, and even her unspoken needs. We were inexplicably connected in ways that I could only feel, but never understand.

Her rage finally reached its peak, like a scene from a movie, as mommy walked over to daddy, who was still sitting in his chair, and slapped him, hard.

His head barely moved as the palm of her hand made contact with the skin on his face. Almost immediately, his cheek turned a bright crimson red. Then he smiled even wider at mommy. She looked down at her hand, as if she couldn't believe what she'd just done. Then she sat down on the kitchen chair, put her head in her hands, and quietly sobbed.

Her rage ended as she wept, pitiful and powerless. She was no match for daddy's unnerving and unwavering determination to stand his ground and not be humiliated. Triumphant, it was the end of the battle, and my little brother and I had witnessed the massacre.

The house became quiet, except for the soft sound of my little brother whimpering next to me. Quickly, I shushed him. I didn't want mommy or daddy to see or hear us. We'd been put to bed hours ago, but we'd both woken up when we heard the yelling. Loud voices were nothing new to us, but the intensity of these yells sounded different. And, this was the first time I saw mommy hit daddy. I was afraid.

Little by little, mommy stopped crying. She lifted her head up and reached for her cigarettes, pulling the long white cylinder carefully from its package. Next, she picked up the package of matches that lay next to the ashtray. Striking the match on the front cover, she lit the cigarette, lifted it to her lips, and inhaled. Letting the smoke out through her pursed lips, she slumped down in her chair and lowered her chin, resting it on her arm that lay on the table. In between drags, she started crying again.

Daddy got up and walked to the bathroom. When he returned, he glanced our way and saw my little brother and I hiding, crouched behind the couch.

As if it was not unusual, he stated matter-of-factly, "Gloria, the kids are awake," as he walked past us and sat back down at the kitchen table. Mommy stopped sobbing and looked over at the couch.

In a firm tone, she told us, "Come out from behind there right now!"

Pleadingly, my little brother looked at me as I pulled him up. We stood next to each other, barely able to see over the top of the couch. Hesitating as we walked to the edge of our turquoise hiding spot, we leaned on the arm of the couch, touching the smooth faux leather with our small hands.

Suddenly, my little brother started to bawl loudly. I put my arm around his shoulder. Dressed in his worn Superman pajamas, I wanted to protect him. He seemed small and vulnerable.

Then mommy began talking. She was still sitting at the kitchen table with daddy. Her lit cigarette sat in the ashtray, half smoked. Composing herself, she stated confidently, "Kids, I need you to make a decision. Who do you want to live with, me or daddy?"

Upon hearing mommy's question, my little brother abruptly stopped crying. We stood next to each other, silently listening as mommy outlined our choices.

Daddy sat stone-faced at the kitchen table while mommy continued, "You can stay here with daddy, or you can come with me."

I looked at mommy and immediately thought, where is she going?

The decision was made in what seemed like an instant, but not by us. My little brother and I would stay in Slidell, with daddy, while mommy traveled to Los Angeles, California for more Scientology auditing and training. That was it! But mommy might as well have told us she was going to the moon. California, although I knew it was a state, sounded like a foreign and faraway unknown land.

Mommy left soon after the heated fight. She was headed to the Advanced Organization in Los Angeles (AOLA), which had recently been established with a crew of Sea Org members, some of whom had been on the ship and at Saint Hill with her. With the opening of the American Saint Hill Organization (ASHO) and (AOLA), Scientology was booming in L.A. It was the new place to go!

My little brother and I were left with daddy until we could all go to L.A., or at least I guess that was the plan. I'm really not sure there was a solid plan. But I'm quite certain that both mommy and daddy agreed that mommy was "the problem," the broken one, and that she would eventually be "fixed" if she just underwent more Scientology auditing and processing.

This definitely appeared to make sense to daddy. Scientology gave him a sense of power and authority over us, and especially over mommy. Anytime she tried to defy him, either verbally or physically, he would quote LRH and tell her how she was "enterbulating" him or the family.

The term, "enterbulating," a made-up Scientology word, meant that you were causing someone harm, or that you were sending out negative energy. Scientologists believe that any problems you're experiencing are always your own fault, and never the consequences of others' actions. It seemed like that was definitely true for mommy.

Before she left, I heard her tell daddy that there was a "break" in their "ARC–Affinity, Reality, and Communication."

She was holding a Scientology book, and reading out loud from it:

> "There must be good affinity (which is to say, affection) between two people before they are very real to each other… Before two people can be real to each other, there must be some communication between them."

Daddy never liked it when mommy quoted L. Ron Hubbard. It seemed that only he was allowed to repeat Scientology words and beliefs.

After she finished reading, mommy told daddy, "Paul, I know we both have withholds and overts."

I'd heard mommy and daddy use these words before, and had

even asked daddy what they meant. He told me it was things you'd done or said that you didn't want anyone to know about.

When I heard mommy tell daddy that they both had withholds and overts, I thought about the secrets that daddy and I both kept from mommy. Withholding our secrets kept them safe, at least for daddy.

. . .

Our house on Monaco Drive was quieter while mommy was away, except when daddy was yelling at us, which was pretty much an everyday occurrence. He had a very bad temper that my little brother and I learned about firsthand while mommy was in California.

It usually started at dinnertime. We were picky eaters. Hamburgers, hot dogs, mac and cheese, the basic foods that all little kids like were our favorites as well. But daddy liked to eat, and he liked mommy's cooking. Unfortunately, though, she was not around to cook. So, daddy took it upon himself to try to prepare her recipes. The results were disappointing, messy, and never as tasty as he wanted them to be.

When I tried to tell daddy that he wasn't making Swiss steak the way mommy made it, which I'd watched her make many, many times, he became furious.

Yelling and screaming at me, "Listen, Pam," he shouted, as he pounded the meat, "I can cook as well as your mother! You just have to follow the recipe. It's not hard! In fact, it's easy!"

"Watch this!" he shouted as he pounded the steak even harder with the wooden mallet. Flour that he'd coated the steak with flew all over the kitchen counter, covering it in a fine white dust.

I knew it looked wrong, but I said nothing. What good would it do anyway?

But soon it was burger night. I sat at our kitchen table, next to my little brother. Daddy sat at the head of the table to my left. Daddy always enjoyed a big juicy burger, or two, loaded with the works: lettuce, tomato, onion, pickles, dripping with mayo, mustard, and ketchup. He usually made some frozen french fries, too, the shoestring skinny kind, to accompany the meal.

I wasn't sure why, but for some reason that night, daddy told me to take off my dress and to just eat in my slip. He told me I dripped too much ketchup on myself while I was eating, and he didn't want to have to wash it. Compliantly, I did what I was told, carefully dipping my French fries in the pool of ketchup on my plate, trying hard not to drip on my white slip.

After dinner, even though I hadn't spilled any ketchup on my slip, or even on my hands, daddy told me to take off my slip and shower with him so I'd be clean for the next school day. Alone and naked with daddy in the shower, his hands held the bar of soap as he covered my body with the bubbly lather. Next, he soaped himself up, paying particular attention to his front and bottom.

I'm not sure where my little brother was during "shower time," probably in his bedroom or the family room playing with his "superhero" dolls. He must have been clean enough.

⸱⸱⸱⸾⸽⸾⸱⸱⸱

LIFE WITHOUT MOMMY

The door to my parents' bedroom was brown and usually closed. But that night, I was on the other side. Daddy's pants were unbuckled and pulled down to the tops of his hairy thighs. His fat white belly spilled over the tops of his legs. As I stared at the ceiling, his hands moved over me. The olive green bedspread undulated like waves underneath me. Everything in our house was olive green or turquoise. I learned to hate these colors.

The long brown dresser where my parents kept their clothes, in closed drawers, was on the other side of the room against the wall. I looked over and stared at it. Mommy's perfume bottle, Tabu, sat next to a small framed picture of the three of us. It was our passport photo. We all looked sad, even though you weren't supposed to smile in passport photos; we looked especially unhappy. As I lay there on the bed, I studied the photo.

Suddenly, the movement stopped. Daddy got up and went into the bathroom. I lay on the bed, quiet and still, then I put my white cotton slip back on. Soft and white with just the tiniest trace of lace around the neck, it had a little pre-tied bow that sat perfectly in the middle, sewn on with a few strands of white thread. I pulled up my white cotton panties. The elastic band sat right below my belly button, tucking away my small belly and genitals for the time being.

Climbing off the bed, I smoothed the bedspread with my small hands. As I walked past the dresser, I glanced at the picture of the three of us, noting again my little brother's sad face, my freckled, unsmiling face, and mommy's resigned look of determination. I felt her stare.

Staring back at her, I imagined asking her, "Where are you? Why did you leave us?"

And then I told myself, "Maybe it's better. You're not here to yell at us. Daddy doesn't have to worry about you throwing hot coffee at him. We don't need you. I'm taking care of daddy without you."

Later, after daddy left the bedroom and went outside to mow the lawn, I snuck back into my parents' bedroom. My little brother was playing with his G.I. Joe dolls, making crashing and banging noises. The dolls were always fighting and driving their jeep into his bedroom walls and over the mountains he made with the pillows from his bed. He didn't hear me as I tiptoed quietly into the bedroom and gingerly closed the door behind me.

I walked over to the dresser and opened one of the drawers. It held clothes that mommy had left behind. Beige, white, and black panties. Folded neatly, one atop the other. Ready for wearing. I touched them, but I didn't unfold them.

My small fingers caressed the nylon. I felt for the elastic waistband hidden on the other side, smooth and soft under my forefinger and thumb; I gently rubbed it.

Closing my eyes, I imagined mommy wearing the beige panties. Even though she was miles away from us, I carefully smoothed the top pair of panties so she wouldn't know I'd touched them.

I closed the drawer, but then decided to open the drawer below it. I felt brave and somewhat defiant. She wasn't there. I could touch her things if I wanted to. I picked up the pink nylon negligee and matching robe that she'd folded in a perfect square and laid in the center of the drawer. A forbidden island of cloth surrounded by the brown wooden sides of the dresser drawer.

I held the negligee up to my petite body, just under my chin, with both hands. It felt soft and thin. Even though it hung down to my ankles, I felt pretty and desirable under the fabric. Mommy was tall. Five-feet eight-inches. "Tall for a woman," she would always say. I moved a few inches to the left so I could see myself in the dresser mirror.

My white cotton slip showed through the thin layer of pink nylon. My pale arms looked small and inconsequential beneath the pink veil. I'm not pretty like mommy, I thought. Resigned to this fact, I folded the negligee back up into a lopsided square, the best folding that I was able to manage, and placed it carefully back in the center of the drawer. Silently, I slid the drawer closed. Daddy wouldn't come looking for me yet. I could still hear the mower outside the bedroom window.

As I turned to leave, I gazed one more time at our passport picture resting on top of the dresser in a black frame. Goodbye, mommy,

I thought. Feeling empowered, I looked in the mirror that rested on top of the dresser.

Staring at my reflection, I stated my resolution, "You're not here, so I can touch your clothes and stand in your bedroom. You're not here to tell me what to do. You're not a good mommy. I will never be like you. I hate you!"

But before leaving the bedroom, I picked up mommy's black bottle of perfume, which sat next to our photo on the dresser. Using my small index finger, I traced the letters and spelled the word in my mind. "T-A-B-U." Then, I slowly pronounced the word phonetically, "Ta-boo." I wondered what it meant.

Even though I was nine years old, I felt my actions and emotions were somehow not childlike. They felt bigger and stronger. Overwhelmed and unyielding to my true powerlessness, I picked up the perfume bottle and unscrewed the top. Placing the opening of the bottle under my nose, I took in the scent. It smelled musky and bad, but also sweet, like flowers that were left in water too long. I closed it up and put it back down next to the picture frame. Opening the bedroom door, I walked out, and shut it quietly behind me. Outside the lawn mower was now silent.

• • •

One afternoon, daddy and I were driving around town in Slidell, one of his favorite activities, driving to nowhere in particular. I sat in the front seat next to him. My little brother was playing at a friend's house, so it was just the two of us. No talking, just driving. Silence and the road, two of daddy's favorite companions.

Suddenly, breaking the silence, daddy asked me a question, something like, "What are you wishing for?" Although not those exact words.

I was shocked! Did he know what I wanted? Could he read my mind? Not sure of what to say, I quickly thought of something. "I wish I didn't have freckles. I don't like them."

Briefly taking his eyes off the road, daddy turned and looked at me with a serious expression on his face.

Speaking in an authoritarian tone he replied, "Well, Pam, if you don't want something, or if you don't like something, like your freckles, you can make a postulate for them to go away, and they will."

I knew a postulate was like a wish in Scientology. I'd heard mommy and daddy talk about "postulating" for more money, often.

Looking down, I mumbled, "Okay," but in my mind I told myself, I don't think a postulate will work. I've been wishing for our family to be different for a very long time, but we aren't.

That was the end of the conversation. But besides wanting a new family, what I really wanted to tell daddy, in the spring of 1968, was that I wanted a training bra. Just like the wonderful cotton collection that Jenny owned. For some reason, Jenny was my new best friend that year.

• • •

When we returned from our trip to England and our adventures on the ship, I was enrolled in fourth grade at the same school I'd left.

Unfortunately, my teacher, Mrs. McMahon, an old Southern woman with grayish silver hair seemed to detest me. I'd arrived midyear into her already-full classroom, and she had her suspicions about where I'd been for the last six months.

Also, she knew that I didn't have a "decent" mother to enroll me in school. I had a very indecent father, a Scientologist. Although I'm pretty sure he never told her that specifically. But in Slidell, being the small Southern town that it was, word traveled quickly.

I think I ended up at Jenny's house after school because daddy didn't have anywhere else for us to go until he got home from work. So, Jenny, who was also motherless—her mom had left her dad when she was little, maybe when she was five or six years old—also had a daddy who was raising her. It was perfect! We were kindred souls. Mother haters, ditched daughters, and daddy lovers.

Jenny possessed the largest collection of oversized stuffed animals that I'd ever seen, from life-sized teddy bears to a hot pink and lime green stuffed Saint Bernard-sized dog. They all sat at attention in a corner of her bedroom. Smaller stuffed animals of varying sizes and colors covered Jenny's bed.

And amazingly, they all wore some version of her white cotton training bra. The two white triangles strapped carefully over their faux fur gave them the appearance of muppet-like porn stars. As we sat amongst the stuffed animals in her bedroom, Jenny, who also sported a white cotton training bra, which she was eager to show me, proudly lifted up her dress.

Imploring me, as she showed off her white cotton bra, she stated, "Just ask your daddy."

Adding, "Show him your buds," as she endearingly called her

nonexistent breasts, in her thick Southern drawl, "And he'll take you to Penney's to pick out all the bras you want. That's what my daddy did."

Lucky you, I thought to myself. You definitely have a different kind of daddy than I have. Needless to say, I remained braless throughout the year.

⟨∞⟩

LEAVING SLIDELL

On photo day at school, since mommy had fled to California, she didn't fix my hair like she usually did. And daddy didn't know how. But it didn't really matter, because my hair was short, like boy hair, while all the other girls in my class had long, pretty, slightly curly hair.

Wearing a new, soft, baby pink dress that I found hanging in my closet after we returned from England, I stood like a statue in the middle row, where the teacher had placed me, with my hands at my sides, trying not to touch anyone. My face was void of emotion, no smile, no frown, no expression.

My Girl Scout classmates were dressed in their green uniform dresses. Sashes filled with badges of accomplishments, they posed confidently with smiles on their faces, and soft, dark green felt berets perched knowingly on their nine- and ten-year-old heads.

After we took our picture, back in our classroom, seated in neat, perfectly aligned rows of desks, feet flat on the floor in front of us, books opened to the correct page in our reading books, we sat silently, waiting for our next instructions.

Calling on me to read, Mrs. McMahon's voice wasn't a kind, "Pamela, would you please read for us today." It was a gotcha moment. She thought I hadn't been paying attention. I was sure she called on me to read because she thought the passage in the story would be too difficult for me. I was certain that her mean-spirited request was intended to find out more about me, and to confirm her supposition that I lacked reading skills.

Looking down at the open book, I felt the hard wooden desk against my body. My voice was soft and quiet, yet audible. I blushed easily and my face turned pink as I read. I felt hot, yet I was confident. I read. I read well. I knew every word. The other children were silent as I read. They too, along with Mrs. McMahon were curious, wondering about me. Where did she go? Why is she back at school? How does she know how to read as well, or better, than we do?

Mrs. McMahon stopped me at the end of the third paragraph.

"That's enough. Thank you, Pamela," she drawled in her Southern nasal accent. "You missed a word, but that's probably because you haven't been in school."

I blushed a deeper shade of pink. My cheeks felt hot, as if they were on fire.

I hated being there with the other children staring at me, and I hated mommy for leaving us. It was her fault that I was back at this school. When Mrs. McMahon wasn't looking, I snuck a hateful glance at her for embarrassing me. Looking back down at my book,

I thought, I will not be sad to leave this school, as I felt her staring back at me.

. . .

Once June arrived, and school was out for the summer, I wondered what the neighbors thought when our furniture was repossessed. The Ethan Allen dining room table with the pecan wood finish, and the gold velvet chairs, along with the stereo console, and the green velvet armchairs and matching couch. Mommy's prized possessions. Loaded into the large furniture truck and driven away in just one day. The other furniture in the house was not as expensive and may have been sold. I'm not sure, but the house was completely empty when we left.

On our last day in this house, daddy sat on the inside window ledge of the empty living room, staring out the window. The ledge was fairly wide, and his large body seemed to be poised comfortably, with one leg crossed over the opposite, leg, forming a rectangle. He wore his usual black pants and a white short-sleeved dress shirt, the two top buttons undone, revealing a white crew neck t-shirt. Black socks, but no shoes. What was he contemplating as he sat there? An ending or a new beginning?

Momentarily, he turned his gaze from the window and looked at me. But no words were spoken. There were no words that daddy could speak that would change what had happened. New owners would someday live here, but our memories would remain in this house, forever locked away.

Days before we moved, daddy told me and my little brother that we were allowed to take one toy with us. Nothing more because he'd already packed our clothes and put the suitcases in the trunk.

Walking down the hall to my empty bedroom, I clutched my one toy, a blonde-haired Barbie that I'd salvaged before the rest were boxed up and given away. My Barbie Dreamhouse and all her clothes and accessories, Midge and Skipper and Ken had all been dumped into the box and taped shut.

It was harder for my little brother. All his G.I. Joes,, their combat uniforms, their jeeps and helicopters, even the replica Apollo 11 spacecraft was put in the box. Hardest of all, though, was listening to him cry as daddy took the superhero models that mommy had carefully and meticulously painted for him off the shelves in his bedroom and boxed them up. Why? Revenge? Or just a practicality. The house needed to be left empty.

Perhaps daddy thought we had too much stuff—"MEST" in the world of Scientology: "Matter, Energy, Space and Time"—so he'd taken care of that. Unfortunately, my little brother and I, although part of my parents' "baggage," weren't as expendable as our worldly belongings.

Yet I believed that I was, at the very least, quiet and somewhat useful. My little brother was always whining about missing mommy. Daddy and I were more practical. It was no use whining about her not being with us. She wasn't coming back to Louisiana. We had to go to her. It was just a reality.

The finality of foreclosure happened without fanfare as we slid into the back seat of our station wagon and headed west, daddy in the driver's seat.

No goodbyes to our neighbors or childhood friends, just glimpses of pine trees and houses passed by the car window as we drove down the street.

Looking out the back seat window, I saw our house one last time, before daddy turned the corner and drove away. Watching the road ahead of us, I wondered about California, but with little thought of seeing mommy again.

PART 2

CALIFORNIA – HERE WE COME!
DRIVING TO LOS ANGELES,
SUMMER OF 1968

We drove through Louisiana. Then across Texas and along the southern borders of New Mexico and Arizona. Through the Mojave Desert. Sand and more sand. Stopping at Stuckey's, a famous landmark, since defunct, after crossing the California border. Then we drove through more desert to Los Angeles. Over 1,900 miles in two days. Quite a road trip!

On the first day of our trip, as we drove from Slidell to the Texas border, daddy decided to pull into the theater parking lot. I looked out the back seat window where my little brother and I sat, bored and tired.

Lined up outside the theater were about twenty, or possibly thirty, black children standing with their black parents, black brothers and sisters, or possibly black friends and cousins. All waiting to see the latest Disney film that had just been released. The marquee of the theater clearly displayed the title, *Mary Poppins*, in large black letters.

I was surprised by the size of the crowd, but also because I'd never seen so many black children or black adults before. Maybe one or two in Louisiana, when we went into New Orleans on a Sunday. But certainly not in my segregated neighborhood or in my segregated elementary school classrooms. Nor in England, or on the *Royal Scotman*. As a general rule, most Scientologists were not black.

As daddy pulled up to the theater, he asked us if we wanted to see the movie. Yes, I thought, but here? I felt unsure in this setting. I'm not sure why. Mostly because I felt different than everyone who was standing in line because of the color of my skin, and because we were only with daddy.

"Okay," he said. "Here's the money to buy the tickets. Go get in line." What? I thought, Get in line without an adult? Isn't he going in with us? I had never gone anywhere without an adult nearby, except for school, and when my little brother and I were in England. But wanting to get out of the car and see the movie, I took the money from his hand, a few dollars, and opened the car door.

Daddy remained in the driver's seat. I told my little brother to get out and follow me. Glad to get out of the car, too, he shuffled over the back bench seat and stretched his little legs to reach the black asphalt of the parking lot.

"Come on," I muttered impatiently. He looked at me with a small scowl on his sleepy face.

"I'm coming," he whined.

Shutting the car door behind him, I took his right hand with my left hand, holding on tight to the dollars that daddy had given me with my other hand. Slowly, we walked to the end of the line of children and adults. I kept my head down as I walked, looking only at the parking lot asphalt under my summer sandals. I watched the numerous black feet that stood in line, shuffling as they waited to buy their tickets. No one spoke to us. We stood silently in the hot midday sun. The box office wasn't open yet.

As we waited, I overheard some children asking their parents if they could get candy, popcorn, and soda. Their requests were met with either silence, or "We ain't got no money for that."

The children kicked at the asphalt and played chase as they waited in line. There were people in front of us and behind us now as the line grew longer. Finally, the line began moving, and we inched our way up to the box office.

A few times, the black family in front of us turned around to stare at us. I wondered what they thought about two little white kids, standing in line at an all-black theatre, without their parents, in an all-black neighborhood. But no one said anything to us. Just looks, some of disdain, but mostly we were regarded with curiosity.

When we reached the box office, I looked up and asked the black man, who I could see through the small window opening, for two tickets.

"Two children?" he asked.

I nodded.

"Three dollars," he replied. Since it was a matinee, the prices were a bit cheaper.

Luckily, daddy had handed me exactly three dollars. I reached up and gave the man the dollar bills I had been holding. They were crumpled and sweaty. He looked at me and my little brother as he handed me two tickets. His face was stern, but his eyes looked sad.

We walked into the theater and gave our tickets to the young black man who stood inside the glass doors that had just opened. Following the crowd of children and families into the red draped theater, I held my little brother's hand tightly, making sure he stayed next to me and didn't wander off.

Some children had convinced their parents to buy popcorn and candy, but most shuffled in without buying anything to eat. Not sure where to sit, I followed a family with two children about the same ages as my little brother and I. Carefully pushing the stained red velvet seat cushion down, I sat next to the mother and motioned for my little brother to sit next to me.

In the dark theater, watching penguins dance while Dick Van Dyke and Julie Andrews sang, my little brother and I were momentarily transported and removed from daddy, and our road trip, to the world of fantasy and make-believe. A very welcome reprieve.

The worn red velvet theater seats felt soft and comfortable against the back of my legs. It was hot outside, but cool inside the movie theater. I watched Dick Van Dyke, funny and kind, as he talked to the children on the screen. I smiled as I watched him dance around with the other chimney sweeps. As I listened to the loud music and the catchy tune, I tapped my foot to the beat.

"*Supercalifragilisticexpialidocious, even though the sound of it is something quite atrocious, if you say it loud enough, you'll always sound precocious...*"

I was mesmerized by Mary Poppins and Bert as they sang and danced.

Afterward, back in the car, as we drove through the desert, I repeated the words over and over in my head, committing them to memory.

I loved to spell, so I broke the word apart into syllables,

"Super – cal – i – fragile – istic – eckspi – al – i – doe – shus."

I wondered what this new word meant. I didn't think it was a Scientology word. And Mary Poppins and Bert were too nice to each other, and the children, to be Scientologists.

•   •   •

We pulled into the parking lot of the motel in New Mexico just as the sun was setting. Orange, pink, yellow, and a dark periwinkle of swirling clouds filled the horizon. Standing next to our car, I gazed at the sunset. I'd never seen one so beautiful, except in books.

As daddy stretched his legs and stared at the neon motel sign, my little brother clutched the metal knight that he'd been allowed to bring on the trip. It belonged to mommy. I don't remember where she bought it, but my little brother liked it.

I'd brought my one Barbie doll, which I left in the back seat of the car. Somehow, she just didn't seem as special without her Barbie dollhouse and the other dolls. Midge, Skipper and Ken. Barbie seemed kind of lost to me without her friends, just like us.

We followed daddy into the motel, and saw a diner inside. We were hungry. Up early in the morning, probably about five am, daddy had driven all day, from Louisiana, until dusk, probably about eight pm. Over 1,000 miles in one day. But daddy was like that. All or nothing. Compulsive, obsessive, and determined.

After checking into the motel, we ate dinner at the small diner, and headed to our room. Daddy surveyed the contents of the motel room. There was one queen-sized bed and one bathroom. He switched on the light to the small bathroom and directed my little brother to take a bath.

Tears began to stream down my little brother's small face as he whined and whimpered that he was too tired, and that he just wanted to watch cartoons. That did it! Exhausted from driving all day, daddy marched over to my little brother and grabbed the metal knight that he'd been tightly clutching. In one swift and purposeful movement, daddy threw the knight powerfully against the motel room wall. Shocked and in a state of disbelief, my little brother wailed even louder.

Fully enraged, daddy screamed, "Stop being such a crybaby! I'm sick and tired of listening to you whine about everything."

He walked over to the metal statue lying on the dirty carpet and picked it up. "This stupid thing. Why did I let you bring it? It's your mother's shit," he yelled as he tossed it onto the bed.

The knight landed on its side. The metal spear that it held in one hand was now slightly bent, as if the knight had been in a battle and lost. My little brother tearfully picked it up and stared at the bent spear.

I stood next to the bed, watching, but at a distance. Daddy was even madder now. His face and neck were red. I knew he was about to explode. He marched over to my little brother and grabbed the knight out of his small hands, again, hurling it into the air.

Like a slow-motion action scene, everything in the room slowed down, daddy's mouth moved slowly and laboriously, mouthing angry words. My little brother's tears dripped like honey from his red-rimmed eyes, and the metal knight turned on its side once again as it glided toward the wall.

• • •

On the last day and night of the trip, as we drove through the desert, my little brother quietly played with his bent knight in the back seat.

Without warning, daddy broke the silence, and said, "Pam, I need you to help me read the signs."

Me? I thought. Why? I knew daddy could read. Why was he asking me to read signs for him? I thought it was maybe a game.

Hungry for a diversion from the long drive, I replied, "Okay."

My little brother seemed content in the back seat, while I sat up front, next to daddy on the bench seat. Since there were no seatbelts, I could crane my neck, and even sit up on my knees and look out the passenger-side window. As I peered out, waiting to spot a sign in the distance, I would ready myself. I wanted to be able to see the sign clearly as we whooshed past it.

"Mo-jaw-vee Desert," I read aloud, proudly yet unknowingly mispronouncing the "ja" syllable.

My Southern education, along with my English-only pronunciation of words, butchered the name, but provided daddy with the information he needed. We were traveling through the desert. His road maps clearly showed a large yellowish-beige area that needed to be crossed in order to get to our destination. We were getting closer.

Tired and weary from driving, daddy's eyes had become fickle over the last year, blurring inadvertently when he needed them to see clearly. A symptom of his Multiple Sclerosis that had yet to be diagnosed.

Finally, after looking at miles and miles of sand, we were in Los Angeles. I continued to read the street signs for daddy as we drove through the city. Butchering and pronouncing names like Cahuenga Boulevard and La Jolla phonetically, like I'd been taught in school. My nine-year-old mouth formed the syllables, "Ca – hoo – wen – gah" and "La – Jaw – la."

We were truly "small town hicks" driving in the "big city." But as daddy's navigator, I sat confidently in the passenger's seat, reading the street signs. I wanted to make sure he knew their names before we passed them, just in case he needed to turn the steering wheel in their direction as he drove us to our final destination, the motel where we would meet mommy.

THE REDWOOD MOTEL

A huge, fake, reddish-brown wagon wheel was precariously positioned on the front side of the motel on Alvarado Boulevard, near downtown Los Angeles. The gigantic letters, The Redwood Motel, were poised next to the wheel just below the roofline of the building.

As daddy turned our car into the small parking lot, my little brother and I both saw the concrete pool, enclosed by a black wrought iron fence and gate. We looked at each other with eyes wide open now after dozing on and off during the morning car ride to the motel. But we didn't dare ask if we could swim.

Getting out of the parked car, my stomach began to tighten. I hadn't seen, or even spoken to, mommy in months. Now, she was just minutes away. I felt unsure, and a bit scared. Fearing a fiery reunion, I held my little brother's hand as we got out of the back seat of the station wagon and climbed up the concrete steps of the motel to the second floor room where she waited for us.

Daddy led the way. He knocked on the motel door. Mommy opened it. But she was not alone. A woman I didn't recognize was in the motel room with her. Daddy kissed mommy on the mouth, then grinned and asked her where the bedroom was, totally ignoring the woman who stood in the middle of the small room.

Mommy held a lit cigarette in her right hand, just as I remembered, between her two slender fingers. She looked thin and pretty. Dressed in a familiar outfit, black slacks and a short-sleeved white cotton blouse that buttoned in the front. Her reddish-brown hair was loosely curled, framing her face, like soft fur. As she bent down and picked up my little brother, I watched her hug him tightly, never letting go of her cigarette.

Silently, I scanned the motel room for the woman and my father. There was no sign of either of them. Where had they gone? The drapes in the room were closed and the room was dark, except for the light from a small desk lamp that was perched on a brown beat-up wooden side table by the loveseat. A console TV sat on the floor against the wall across from the loveseat.

As mommy put my little brother down, she finally looked over at me. Our eyes met. I could feel my heart thumping in my chest. I thought to myself, I hate you! Why did you leave us? She reached for me and I willed myself not to cry.

We hugged briefly as she wrapped one arm around my shoulders. I loosely placed my small arm around her waist. Her body felt soft through her thin white blouse. Cigarette still intact between her fingers, we released each other. She looked down at me as she took a long drag and then exhaled slowly. Smoke and her words intermingled in the dark air of the shabby motel room. "I've missed you kids," she told us.

Yeah, right. Well, we haven't missed you, I thought.

The woman, my mother's Scientology "escort," had momentarily left the room, allowing us to reconnect as a family. She now stood quietly near the curtains. Finally, she spoke up and asked, "Well kids, how about watching some cartoons while your parents have some time alone?"

My little brother and I gave each other a sideways glance and replied simultaneously, "Sure."

We were always glad to be able to escape into the world of Wile E. Coyote and the sneaky Road Runner. Without hesitating, we quickly sat down on the dirty carpet in front of the TV set while the woman turned it on and found a cartoon channel. It was probably about three in the afternoon and there were only a few choices. The woman sat down on the loveseat, lit a cigarette, and gazed at the TV set with us.

Lost in the antics of Wile E. Coyote as he tried to outsmart the Road Runner, my little brother and I were entertained. Tired of being in the car, we welcomed this reprieve. After about fifteen or twenty minutes, Wile E. was blown up by dynamite, again, and I told the woman that I needed to go to the bathroom.

She said, "Sure, honey. It's right over there, next to the bedroom."

I walked past the bedroom door, which was slightly cracked open, on my way to the bathroom. Nonchalantly, I peered through the open crack, and saw mommy, half-dressed, lying on the bed. She held a menthol Kool cigarette in her right hand between her long index finger and her middle finger. Immediately, I noticed that she wasn't wearing any pants, only her white cotton blouse, which was still buttoned.

Up until then, I'd never seen mommy without clothing. The most I'd ever seen of her body was when she wore her pink nylon nightgown. It was slightly see-through, and if the lighting was just right, I could see her nipples and her pubic hair through the thin nylon material. Like when she sat at our old kitchen table in the morning with her cup of black coffee and her cigarette.

As I peered into the bedroom, I couldn't see daddy in the bed. Maybe he was in the bathroom. Even though I was almost ten years old, I didn't really get that my parents had just had sex after being apart for months. I only knew that it felt uncomfortable for all of us to be in this dumpy motel room with mommy in the bedroom, half-naked,, as my little brother and I sat on the dirty olive green shag carpet in front of the TV watching cartoons.

Soon, mommy got dressed and came out into the room with my little brother and me. She plopped down onto the dirty orange couch. My little brother got up from where he was sitting on the carpet and walked over to her. She reached out for him and motioned for him to sit next to her. He smiled and climbed onto the couch, snuggling in close to mommy. She casually threw her arm around his shoulders and lit up another cigarette. They looked content.

Feeling left out, I got up and pretended to walk toward the bathroom. As I passed the open bedroom door, I glanced in and saw daddy zipping and buckling his black pants. He held his black belt in his hands, wrapping it around his pudgy waistline as he pulled it through the belt loops, eventually meeting the gold-colored buckle in the front. Then he put the gold prong through the hole and cinched it closed. His movements were familiar.

I watched intently as he turned around to sit down on the bed to put on his shoes. He had kept his black socks on. As he looked up, he saw me standing outside of the bedroom door in the small space between the sitting area and the bathroom. Daddy smiled at me. He looked happy. I wanly smiled back then put my head down and walked back to where my little brother and mommy sat cozily next to each other.

Mommy was curled up on the couch with a cigarette between her lips, her arm still loosely draped over my little brother's shoulder. Watching them, I felt sad, jealous of their love, and envious of the closeness mommy had just shared with daddy. In that moment, I despised her for not loving me the way that I needed to be loved, and I was angry with her for taking daddy away from me.

Not surprising, our reunion with mommy hadn't turned out the way I wanted. Secretly, in my private fantasy world, I'd imagined a different version of our family's reunion, one that was more emotional, complete with mommy sobbing about how much she'd missed me and my little brother.

I imagined her holding my hand as we sat on the loveseat, saying, "Oh, honey! It's so good to see you. I've missed you so much!"

Then she would stroke my hair and hold me tightly as I cried against her warm body. But that was fantasy and this was our reality.

⁂

MAKING NEW FRIENDS

In September of 1968, after moving to California, my little brother and I walked onto a downtown inner city Los Angeles elementary campus where Clanton 14, the local Mexican street gang, marked its territory on the stucco beige walls of Tenth Street Elementary School.

Neither my little brother nor I had any idea what a street gang was, nor what Clanton 14 meant. We were lost, both culturally and emotionally, immersed in a land where both Spanish and English were spoken on the playground and in the classrooms. Spanish was a language we'd never heard before.

With my short, kind of Twiggy-meets-Peter-Pan, pixie haircut, without the cute wispy edges to frame my face, my mousy brown hair lay flat and uneven on my small head. Wearing a gray and white paisley print sweater dress with an attached silver medallion, I did

NOT look like anyone else at this new school. We were just two new, unknown white kids who stood out like ghosts in a sea of brown faces. I'm sure my Mexican classmates had no idea what to think of me or my little brother.

Daddy had driven us to school for our first day, and walked onto the campus with us, which drew stares from the children we passed. Only a few other parents seemed to be on campus, and not one of them was white. Daddy definitely stood out. After leaving us on the playground, he watched us from outside the chain-link fence as we were told by teachers, who'd been assigned to the playground, where to line up.

I walked my little brother to his line first, afraid he might start crying, and that I'd be pulled out of class to comfort him, just as I had been at the Episcopal school in England. I left him standing in line sandwiched between two small brown-skinned boys. I told him I would see him at lunchtime, hoping that was true.

Walking back to where I'd been told to line up, on the other side of the playground, I felt a bit nervous, but also excited about the prospects of a new school. I also felt relieved to finally be leaving the apartment we'd moved into after our brief stay at the Redwood Motel. All I could think of, as I stood waiting quietly in line, was that it felt good to be away from mommy. Living without her for so long had begun to feel normal.

My teacher, Mr. Vogel, was beginning his first year of teaching in the Los Angeles Unified School District. With black-rimmed glasses that framed his eyes, and a soft, yet firm manner of speaking to his students, he created a warm, and welcoming environment for us. Gangs and inner-city poverty lurked just outside the gates of our school, but within the walls of our classroom, he made learning fun and interesting.

After only several days of school, he noted that I could read well, and he accelerated me to a reading group of about four students who were also good readers. We enjoyed listening to each other, especially when Mr. Vogel came to sit with us. He didn't praise us for our reading skills, but instead questioned us, asking us to explain what we had read, and to write about it. I felt valued. He seemed to care about my thoughts and what I had to say. So different from my parents, who wanted me to keep their secrets.

Javier, Rafael, Joey, and Gerardo, who were eleven- and twelve-year-old prepubescent boys and first-generation Mexican immigrant children, surprisingly chose to be friends with me. They were all smart and funny. Joey was the cocky one, thinking he was "all that" because he had an American name; he was smart in an "I am better than you" way, not in a "so glad that I found another smart person to talk to" way.

Both Javier and Joey were short. But despite his height, Javier looked almost adult-like. He wore a white shirt and black pants to school every day, which made him seem "dressed-up" compared to the other kids. His shiny black faux patent leather shoes protruded from underneath his slightly-too-long pant legs. When he walked, you could sometimes catch a glimpse of white athletic socks peeking out from the tops of his shoes. His jet-black hair was slicked down and parted on the side, and his dark eyes seemed to twinkle when he laughed. He was clearly Joey's devoted friend and sidekick. They were inseparable.

Rafael was the sensitive, shy friend who listened more than he spoke. He traveled with Joey and Javier from corner to corner on the large asphalt playground, sometimes hanging back just a little, waiting and watching. I liked Rafael. I found him elusive, and a bit mysterious. He was taller than the other boys, with curly light-brownish hair and beautiful, dark, long-lashed, deep-brown eyes. His mouth was soft. When he spoke, his words seemed to be chosen carefully and with thoughtful consideration.

One day, in our sixth grade classroom, during an assigned art project, we drew and colored on large white sheets of construction paper. Sitting catty-corner to each other at the table, Rafael and I shared the space, our papers spread out in front of us. It was the first time that I saw his exquisite drawings.

He was an artist. The real kind, like my little brother, who seemed to be able to draw anything without even trying. Their artistic gift just oozed out of them. Like having a magical hand that came to life when you picked up a pencil. Gazing at his artwork, I felt both envy and respect for Rafael.

As we continued to draw and color, the usual rule of working quietly, without talking, was challenged. It started with just two students who were seated across the table from each other. In hushed voices, we tested the limits. No rebuffs occurred, so our young voices got louder. Still no signal from Mr. Vogel to cease and desist. We were free to engage in dialogue and childish banter, even laughing and giggling.

I don't remember exactly what was said, and by whom, but Rafael cocked his head back and let out a laugh that sounded almost musical. From deep within him, a melodious sound emerged. It poured from his open mouth, blanketing our corner of the classroom. Holding my crayon carefully between my fingers, I bent my head and giggled softly to myself. Rafael had given me permission to feel happy.

. . .

A few weeks later, Alice, a girl in our class, also befriended me. Our friendship began not in the classroom, but on the concrete steps of our school. After showing me how to sneak out the back gate, which was attached to the chain-link fence, we quickly walked into the corner liquor store and market. Speaking rapidly to the store clerk in Spanish, she bought us thinly-sliced lunch meat sandwiches and potato chips. Grabbing the brown paper bags that held our lunch, we slinked back onto campus, all within about five minutes.

Alice was slightly older and definitely more street-smart than most of our classmates. She was like a tour guide in a foreign land, showing me all the side streets and tucked away corners of a city I might be visiting, that only a local might know about.

I liked Alice. She was everything I was not on the outside and everything I feared might be true about myself on the inside. My alter ego. She was not particularly smart in school, or at least she didn't care to show her intelligence. She participated in learning from a distance as she sat on the fringes of our classroom caste system. She wasn't naughty or openly defiant, just passively noncompliant.

One day, while we sat on the steps of one of the school buildings, facing the back side street that bordered the school, I asked Alice if I could come over to her house to play. She looked at me intently, her brown almond-shaped eyes, framed by straight dark-brown hair that hung down the sides of her face, seeming filled with a hint of sadness. As she chewed and swallowed a bite of her storebought sandwich, she lowered her head and looked down at the black asphalt of the playground. "You can't come to my house," she said definitively.

"Why?" I asked.

"Because you're white," she casually responded.

"I know. But why does that matter?" I replied. I didn't understand what she was telling me. I thought we were friends.

"I'm Mexican and you're not. My father isn't going to let me play with you. He only likes Mexicans," she explained.

"Can't you tell him I'm Mexican?" I asked.

Alice stood up and balled up the paper wrapping from her sandwich. She casually walked over to the metal trash can next to the building and tossed it in. I didn't know whether she was coming back or if I should get up and follow her.

I stood up, holding my half-eaten sandwich in my hands, surrounded by its white paper wrapping. She turned and walked back to where we'd been sitting. Looking me straight in the eyes, she stated, as if she was describing common, known facts, like the clouds and the sun in the sky, "You are a gringa, you have white skin. We can't be friends."

I wanted to cry but I didn't. Alice was tough. I wanted to be as tough as she was. I wanted to be able to state my feelings and facts as simply as she did. I felt angry. Why wasn't my skin brown like hers? Why did I have white skin when almost everyone at this school had brown skin? Why did I have to be different?

When I got home from school that day, I stood in the middle of the living room and bravely stated what I wanted to mommy, who was seated in a cross-legged position on the carpet in front of the TV.

"I don't want white skin. I want to have brown skin."

She looked up at me, somewhat puzzled. "Did something happen at school today?" she asked.

I was NOT going to tell her about Alice or what she'd said to me. That was my secret, along with all my other secrets that I never told her.

"No," I replied adamantly. "I just want brown skin like everyone else at school."

Barely acknowledging my response, she mumbled to herself, then turned back toward the TV, pursed her lips around the end of her cigarette, and took a long drag. That was the end of the conversation.

Yearning to fit in at my new school, I decided that once again, it was her fault that I didn't. In my mind, just an additional reason to hate her.

SIXTH GRADE
GRADUATION PARTY

Yet even without brown skin, I found myself genuinely accepted and liked by most of my classmates. At the end of sixth grade, I was thrilled to be invited to a graduation party by Sylvia, one of the popular Mexican girls in our class. She was pretty and thin, with shoulder-length jet-black hair and large brown eyes that were covered with dark black eyelashes. Sylvia had a bubbly personality, and she loved being the center of attention.

One day after school, as my little brother and I were walking out the school gates, Sylvia stopped me and asked, "Pam, I'm having a graduation party on Saturday. It's at my house. Can you come? Everyone in our class will be there, especially Gerardo."

She looked at me and smiled knowingly.

Sylvia had been watching Gerard, who chose to use his

Americanized name, and me in class and on the playground. He was taller than most of the boys, with curly light-brown hair and beautiful greenish eyes that he kept hidden behind glasses. He was a bit bookish and very sweet-natured. I definitely had a crush on him.

Shyly, I looked down at the ground. Inside my chest, it felt like my heart was beating too fast.

I stammered, "Sure. Where do you live?"

Sylvia winked at me and assured me that she would give me an invitation with all the details. "Bye, it will be lots of fun!"

Sylvia giggled as she turned and ran out of the school gate and down the street toward a group of girls who had been waiting for her. I followed her with my eyes as she yelled, "Wait for me! Esparame!" to her friends.

After walking home with my little brother, I casually told mommy that I'd been invited to a graduation party.

Her reaction to the invitation was typical.

"That's nice. Who's having the party?" she asked.

"Just a girl named Sylvia," I casually replied.

No further questions.

Sylvia's house was close to our school, which my little brother and I walked to daily. Our route was easy to remember. From our apartment in downtown L.A., we walked down Bonnie Brae Avenue one block to Olympic Boulevard and headed east. Then we walked down Olympic, which was a busy street, for quite a few blocks until we passed Union Avenue. It was only about one more block further until we turned right and finally reached our school. It took us about fifteen minutes, if we walked quickly.

Each morning, on our way to school, we passed one of the big office buildings on Olympic Boulevard. I liked watching the business people as they entered. The men were dressed in their business suits, and the women wore pretty dresses and high heels. I wondered what they did all day.

There was also a restaurant that was always busy, both in the morning and in the afternoon. As we passed by it each day, I entertained myself by looking in the window to see what the people were eating. It always looked the same. Coffee and breakfast in the morning and sandwiches in the afternoon.

Sylvia's party was going to start after school, so I'd only have to walk a few blocks from school to her house. But I knew I needed a ride home because the party might not end until after dinner. I didn't want to walk home by myself in the dark, so I decided to tell daddy about the party, and he didn't seem to mind driving to pick me up afterward.

Mommy didn't drive after we arrived in Los Angeles, mainly because we only had one car that daddy drove to work every day. Daddy also did most of the shopping too, driving us to the grocery store while mommy stayed home in our apartment. I didn't know it at the time, but this was the beginning of her agoraphobia.

The day of the party, I walked to Sylvia's house with a few other kids from our class who'd been invited. We chattered about school as we walked up the short cement walkway to Sylvia's house. She greeted us at the front door.

"Hi! Come in," she bubbled as she opened the door and motioned for us to follow her.

Sylvia wore a light-blue party dress that was quite short, revealing her skinny brown legs. As she skipped through her house, her dress shimmered and sparkled in all the right places.

Cautiously, we followed her into the small front room that was filled with a floral couch and fabric chairs. The couch was covered in plastic, which I'd never seen before. A beautifully crocheted, multi-colored blanket lay across the back of the couch, covering part of the plastic. It was a very tidy room. It looked untouched, as if no one ever really sat on the furniture.

We continued to follow Sylvia into the kitchen, which was small. Nestled against the walls were a sink, a refrigerator, an oven, and a stovetop for cooking. Counter space was limited. The smell of freshly made tortillas, beans, rice, and meat wafted toward us as we walked in.

Turning to a woman who looked older than mommy, Sylvia introduced me in Spanish.

"Esta es mi amiga de la escuela. Se llama Pam."

The woman turned from the stove where a large pot of something fragrant was boiling. She wore a plain, light-colored cotton dress with a collar, covered by a long white apron that was tied around her middle. She wasn't chubby, but definitely she had more meat on her bones than mommy, who was skinny. The woman's dark hair was loosely tied up in a bun on the top of her head. Holding the spoon, she'd been using to stir the contents of the pot in one hand, she wiped the other hand on her white apron. As she turned from the stove, she looked down at me, smiled, and stated, "Mucho gusto."

Sylvia told me, "She's glad to meet you."

I nodded and smiled shyly. This home and kitchen were nothing like the apartment we lived in, nor the houses we'd lived in before moving to California. It seemed so warm and friendly. I immediately felt accepted.

Sylvia continued to lead us through the kitchen where her mother was cooking along with two other women. One of the women resembled Sylvia's mother, and the other woman had gray hair. I assumed they were Sylvia's aunt and grandmother.

They moved about the kitchen, stirring pots, taking food out of the oven, and conversing in Spanish. I didn't understand what they were saying, but I could tell by the tone of their voices, and their movements, that they were happy as they cooked and prepared the food for our party.

Sylvia guided us out of the small kitchen and out the back door, down two concrete steps to the small backyard. The yard included a patch of green grass, a side yard where an empty metal clothesline stood, and a concrete rectangle with tables and chairs set up around it.

The tables were covered with paper tablecloths. Paper plates, napkins, and plastic utensils were neatly stacked on one side. Twinkle lights, like the kind you put on a Christmas tree, had been strung along the top of a white tent that surrounded the concrete rectangle.

Standing in Sylvia's backyard, down the street from our elementary school, listening to my classmates laughing and talking, I saw a sea of faces that I knew from our playground and the four walls of our classroom. Now, here they all were, standing in their Sunday best, ready for an afternoon and evening of partying. Although at eleven and twelve years old, it was all innocent fun.

I watched as my classmates ate plates of freshly-made tacos, beans, rice, and tortillas, and told each other silly school jokes. The girls huddled on one side of the party tent while the boys gathered on another side, close to the food.

As the sun began to set, the dusky sky and the twinkle lights transformed the calm afternoon into a beautiful June evening. From the radio, which had been brought outside and set up on one of the tables, Creedence Clearwater Revival sang:

"Early in the evenin' just about supper time... Down on the corner, out in the street... the Poor Boys are playin' bring a nickel, tap your feet...."

When the song started, all the girls ran to the concrete rectangle and began dancing. Their feet moved rhythmically and in sync. Dance steps created for this song, one they'd heard so often they'd memorized every word, which they sang loudly and in unison.

From my spot by the table, I watched the girls, wanting to join them.

Finally, Sylvia glanced my way and saw that I wasn't dancing. She ran over to me and grabbed my hand.

"Come on, Pam. You need to dance with us."

"But I don't know how," I stammered.

"I'll teach you," she gushed as she pulled me toward my classmates.

Embarrassed, I looked down at her feet as she performed the dance steps. She moved her shiny black shoes slowly and purposefully for me to copy. But I was quite uncoordinated. I had no idea how to dance the way she did.

As Sylvia prodded me to copy her movements, I tried my best, faltering and wishing the song would end. Finally, it did. The girls giggled and clapped as they left the concrete. I followed them over to the table laden with food. Carefully, I placed a flour tortilla on my plate and scooped a spoonful of rice next to it. I wasn't sure if I would like it, but I wanted to blend in and not draw attention to myself.

As the sky grew a bit darker, in the distance, over the rooftops of the other small houses, you could see a faint touch of pink mixed with gray. The music from the radio continued to play, interspersed with banter from the popular radio station, KHJ. The DJ—the Real Don Steele—played, played all the latest hits and top-ten songs on the music charts.

Soon, a slower song started playing. The boys started to fidget as they heard the music. In groups of two and three they casually walked over to the girls and asked them to dance. The girls smiled coyly as they followed the boys to the concrete dance floor. Placing their hands on the girls' waists, the girls reciprocated and gingerly placed their hands on their partner's shoulders. Shuffling to the music, their feet bumped gently against each other.

Not everyone was dancing, though. A few girls and boys remained by the tables, including me. Out of the corner of my eye, as I pretended to eat the rice on my plate, I saw two boys nudge Gerardo. He blushed and quickly glanced over at me. The boys pushed him in my direction and he reluctantly walked over.

The girls, who were standing near me, whispered loudly. "He's coming to ask you to dance."

I felt the heat rise from my neck. My cheeks burned. I was sure they were a bright red. I hoped he wouldn't notice.

Taller than most of the kids in our class, he stood in front of me. As he looked down, he asked, "Do you want to dance?"

Panic and excitement enveloped me as I quietly replied, "Sure."

Surprised by my response, he smiled, turned, and walked toward our dancing classmates. I followed him. Stepping from the grass to the cement, he held out his hand to me. I took it. His touch felt warm, not sexual, but safe.

As he placed his hands on my waist, I tried to reach his shoulders by stretching my arms, but they fell short. I rested my hands on his skinny biceps as we slowly moved our feet and swayed to the music. Incredulous, I couldn't believe that I was really dancing with him. I didn't want the song to end.

As the music continued, Sylvia's relatives, along with a few other parents, left the kitchen. They gathered next to the steps at the back of the house, proudly watching their children. Sons and daughters who had learned to speak English, allowing them to begin their successful assimilation into American culture. Their parents' smiles conveyed their pride and the hope that they held for them. Aspirations of a better life.

When daddy arrived to pick me up, I said goodbye to everyone, wondering if I'd ever see them again, now that school was out for the summer.

Walking through the kitchen to the front room, Gerardo looked at me and said, "Bye, Pam. See you in junior high."

I hoped it would be true.

APARTMENT NEIGHBORS

S hortly after our brief stay at the Redwood Motel, where we reunited with mommy, we moved into a ground floor apartment at 909 South Bonnie Brae Avenue in downtown Los Angeles. I'd never lived in an apartment except when I was a baby in Washington, D.C., which I don't remember. Meeting and watching our apartment neighbors proved to be both interesting and educational.

Aramita was a beautiful, tall African American woman who lived in one of the second floor apartments above ours. She and mommy were friends, or at least that was my impression.

I'm not sure if she was a Scientologist, but mommy liked to visit Aramita and sometimes brought me with her. I loved watching Aramita float through her apartment wearing colorful caftans. Her huge dark-black Afro surrounded her head and swayed softly as she moved. Aramita exuded both calmness and serenity.

Mommy and Aramita usually smoked and talked at the kitchen table while I sat close by, listening to them. I'm not sure why, but Aramita always seemed genuinely interested in mommy and in what she had to say. I watched as she nodded and kindly responded, "Yes, I can see that," when mommy told her something that didn't seem very interesting at all. Or sometimes she'd say, "That's quite a story," when mommy shared one of her long stories that I'd heard before.

But I liked visiting Aramita, because while she and mommy talked, I could watch her teenage daughter, who was petite and artistic, draw huge wide-eyed doll faces. She was probably about fifteen or sixteen years old. Quiet and withdrawn. Rarely speaking, except once, when she sought my praise and asked, "Do you like my drawings?"

To which I sheepishly replied, "Yes," amazed that she would even care what I thought.

• • •

Directly above us, in a corner apartment, also on the second floor, lived Doreen, and her mother Charity, both Scientologists. Doreen was only twelve years old, but she looked so much older and grown-up to me. Her swagger and confidence were tangible as I watched her walk down the concrete staircase to the first floor. Standing tall and lean, her long blonde hair flowed over her shoulders and down her back. She seemed both important and proud.

But not long after we moved into our apartment, Doreen left

Los Angeles and boarded the *Royal Scotman*, the same ship we had sailed on, although it had been renamed the *Apollo*. On the ship, Doreen was quickly chosen to serve as one of several young girls who were given the exclusive title of "the Commodore's Messengers," a coveted position that Hubbard created when he assumed the title of "Commodore." The "Messengers" had many duties, the most important of which included delivering Hubbard's verbal tirades and "ethical punishments" to other Sea Org members who were not performing their duties according to his wishes.

Years later, Doreen spoke about being chosen: *"I was thrilled to death. It was what I had wanted from day one. LRH was my hero. We'd always had his picture hanging on the wall at home and we listened to his tapes all the time. I was his greatest fan."*

Yet, tragically, Doreen's young life was cut short when she died in her early thirties in a horseback riding accident, after finally leaving Scientology.

• • •

One of our more interesting neighbors, who also lived upstairs, was named Leslie. I watched in awe the first time I saw Leslie emerge from his apartment. He wore white high heels and a slightly-sheer blouse that stretched tightly across his bosom, exposing dark-black cleavage.

A hot-pink mini skirt revealed long, slender legs. His shoulder-length dark-black hair, a synthetic wig, framed his feminine facial features, which were accentuated by long black false eyelashes and red lipstick. Smiling as he swung his hips back and forth, he walked across the open concrete hallway to the elevator. His toothy smile dazzled.

"Hi, there," he said as he spotted me gawking. "What's your name, honey? I'm Leslie."

Dumbfounded, I quietly whispered, "Pam," as I watched him enter the elevator and push the G button to the garage with his long perfectly polished red fingernail.

A gold bracelet hung loosely on his thin wrist, and gold rings with shiny gems populated several fingers on both hands. As the doors closed, he winked, smiled, and waved. I stood at the closed elevator door for a few seconds, contemplating my exchange with Leslie.

Later that day, I told, Mark, our next-door neighbor, and the apartment manager's son, about the encounter. As I described "her" to Mark, he silently listened.

When I was finished, he looked straight at me, hands on both hips as he sneered, "Leslie is a man, not a woman."

Defiantly, I told him that he was wrong as I described our encounter in detail.

He looked at me, full of disdain.

"He's a transvestite," he scoffed.

"What's that?" I asked.

"It's a man who dresses up like a woman," he replied all-knowingly.

"Why?" I asked innocently.

He just rolled his eyes at me and turned to walk away. I considered his explanation, but remained curious. Leslie was definitely a new and interesting character to be watched.

. . .

As soon as school let out for the summer, our daily apartment building ritual began, playing Milton Bradley's The Game of Life. Sitting on the hot concrete that surrounded the swimming pool, our friend, Richard, and Mark, had just set up the gameboard. It was ten o'clock in the morning on a hot July day, and there was no shade covering to be found.

Dressed in a loosely-fitted t-shirt and a pair of shorts, I sat cross-legged next to my little brother on the cement, ready to flick the spinner that determined my daily fate. However, for all intent and purposes, my little brother was just a placeholder, because we needed four people to play. Most of the time he just walked around or played with his G.I. Joe dolls that mommy had recently purchased, replacing the ones that daddy had given away in Louisiana.

Competitive and focused, Mark played a serious game. He was cynical by nature, and usually made disparaging remarks about us or our life paths.

"Pam, are you really going to have that many children?"

And "Well, that's certainly not going to help you get rich," he uttered sarcastically as we twirled the spinner and moved our little plastic cars around the gameboard.

Mark was an eleven-year-old French-Canadian Catholic. He looked fit and well-groomed in his summer wardrobe of denim shorts and a mostly-fitted white t-shirt. Mark always wore flip-flop sandals that showed off his perfectly-manicured toes and toenails. He never took his sandals off, abhorring the thought of getting his feet dirty on the dusty concrete.

Richard, on the other hand, was disheveled and a bit wild. His small unkept Afro framed his ten-year-old face, and an impish, toothy grin revealed yellowish, capped teeth, whenever his lips parted. Richard's wardrobe included about three different shirts: blue, green, and yellow, all variations on a plaid theme. Daily, he wore the same pair of black pants, dark-colored socks, and old tennis shoes.

Playing with Richard was always entertaining because he was so hilarious and animated. Every time he spun the dial he jumped up and ran around the concrete patio that surrounded the apartment swimming pool.

After completing his lap around the pool, he sat back down and exclaimed, "Here we go! I feel my life movin' in the right direction. Watch out world! Here I come! Are you ready for me? Can you dig it?"

We all laughed so hard each time that Richard took his turn. I loved the sound of his laugh! Rich, real, and heartfelt. And I felt a connection with him. His mother, who was single, worked full-time, so both Richard and I were basically left on our own throughout the summer. The only difference, and perhaps quite a notable one, was that I had to keep an eye on my little brother while daddy worked and mommy was busy with Scientology.

THE PHOTO SHOOT

One day, later that summer, as I swam in the apartment swimming pool, mommy walked over to the edge where I was treading water and casually said, "Pam, did I tell you that John was coming over today to take your picture?"

Um, no, I thought, but responded, "Okay."

I wasn't sure who John was, but I liked the idea that someone, especially a grown man, wanted to take my picture. Although at twelve years old, I really just wanted to keep swimming. So I stayed in the pool and swam, making my way down to the bottom of the pool.

As I pushed up with my feet, propelling myself six feet to the surface, I imagined being free. Free from my family, free from our life in the apartment, and free from Scientology and its continuous roller coaster of moving and relocating.

Every time we moved, Scientology was the reason, or at least that is how it appeared to me as a child. However, money was more likely the reason. I knew Daddy had to work in order to provide for our family, but also to pay mommy's Scientology bills. But mommy definitely didn't seem better after this move. She seemed more distant and unhappy. I wished often that our family could escape from the strange world of Scientology.

Under the water, I felt that freedom. After submerging myself for at least sixty seconds, I swam toward the top. Once my head broke through, I gasped for air above the chlorine-blue surface of the water.

Wiping the water from my eyes, I saw mommy at the edge of the pool, looking angry, exasperated, and annoyed.

"Pam, you need to get out of the pool and get dressed. John is waiting for you!"

Standing next to mommy was the photographer, the man called John. He wore clothing very similar to daddy's wardrobe, including a short-sleeved white dress shirt that revealed his white undershirt at the neck. A belted pair of black pants, black socks, and black shoes completed his outfit.

But John appeared to be older than daddy, with black hair peppered with gray. In one hand he held a black Nikon camera. In the other hand he carried what looked like a small black suitcase with two gold locks on the top next to the handle.

I swam over to the metal ladder on the deep side of the swimming pool, my summer oasis away from my little brother, away from mommy, and away from our reality. In my turquoise-blue underwater world, I reigned over my own destiny.

As I climbed up the stairs, and stood on the cement, water

dripped off my pale-blue paisley print ruffled bikini bottom and matching top, forming a small puddle around my bare feet. I turned to look at John and mommy.

He looked down at me and smiled a fake adult smile. The kind of smile that teachers give you when they must pretend that they like you, but they really don't. The kind of smile that conveys contempt or pity.

Like a spy, I watched mommy, Kool cigarette perched between her long, slightly-tanned fingers, her eyes covered by dark sunglasses as she smiled, talked, and laughed with John. Dressed in her standard 1960s uniform, a white short-sleeved cotton blouse and a pair of black polyester pants, she stood barefoot, her pink toenail polish chipped off at the ends.

She hadn't curled her short hair last night the way she usually did, rolling it up with sponge rollers and sleeping on them under a shower cap. Her hair looked more like a short shag than her usual coifed and teased hairdo. She looked messy.

Walking over to the chaise lounge chair with vinyl straps, I picked up the thin cotton beach towel covered with fake palm trees and the word California printed in the middle. A souvenir from our road trip. The warmth of the towel, which had been sitting in the sun, felt comforting against my wet skin as I wrapped it around my wet shoulders. Water dripped from my hair, and my eyes were red-rimmed from swimming underwater in the chlorine.

That day, I remember feeling old. Older than just twelve, as if I were an adult, one of them. Isn't that what Scientology preached? I had heard my parents say often that children were really just thetans, like old souls, but in small bodies. I had started to believe it was true.

Walking into our apartment, I went into the bathroom and peeled off my wet bathing suit. Wrapped in just my towel, I hurried into the bedroom that I shared with my little brother, who was off playing Superman somewhere, lost in his own separate and imaginary reality, oblivious to the world of Scientology.

I tugged the blousy yellow dress that mommy had made for me over my head, and pulled my arms through the thin material that she had sewn onto the bodice. The buttons at the cuffs matched the three opaque white buttons that stood at attention down the front of the polyester garment. I tried to reach the button in the back that would cinch the thin white-and-yellow-dotted Swiss fabric collar closed, but my arms were too short. I left it open.

After getting dressed, I opened the bedroom door and walked back into the bathroom. I crookedly parted and brushed my wet, chlorine-infused shoulder-length hair as I watched my reflection in the medicine cabinet mirror.

The edges of the cabinet were rusty, and parts of the mirror were gray and veiny. I saw myself not for who I was, but for who I wanted to be, whom I imagined, whom I dreamed of becoming. Prettier, sexier, alluring, and definitely older. I wished I was thirteen. That was the magic number.

Leaving the bathroom, barefoot, I walked onto the olive green shag carpeting in the living room of our apartment. The green yarn protruding from between my toes reminded me of rough, fuzzy worms of different sizes and lengths all huddled together, fearing they would be smashed by feet, with nowhere to hide.

The sparse furniture in our apartment didn't belong to us. It was standard 1960s rental apartment décor. A cheap orangish-colored arm chair with dark stains on the arms sat nestled in the shag carpeting on one end of the room near the console TV set. The brown-and-green-striped couch sat against the opposite wall.

The room was dark, cave-like. Mommy never opened the door or the curtains, which added to our prison-like existence. I looked around the apartment for her, but she hadn't come back inside. I opened the front door and saw them, mommy and John, still standing outside near the pool chatting.

As I walked over to where they stood, mommy stated, somewhat impatiently, "Pam, we've been waiting for you. John, this is my daughter, Pam. I'll let you two get started."

At that, she coyly smiled at John. Then she turned around and walked back to our apartment. I watched her as she opened the apartment door, went inside, and shut the door behind her. I was stunned. I'm not sure why, but I was.

I felt shy and annoyed. Why was she leaving me alone with this grown man who I didn't even know?

"Hi," I stammered in a very soft voice that was almost a whisper.

John placed his hand on the small of my back, just above where the top of my white cotton underwear sat underneath the yellow dress.

"What a pretty dress," he cooed as he guided me over to a chaise lounge chair near the pool.

I whispered, "My mother made it."

"Oh, I didn't know Gloria could sew." He chuckled as if her

ability to engage in any activity other than Scientology training and auditing was preposterous.

John sat down on the lounge chair and motioned for me to sit next to him. His body covered most of the vinyl straps on the chair, leaving me a small space to sit. His leg, covered by his black pants, touched my bare, slightly-tanned thigh. He rested his hand on my also-bare freckled knee.

"So, your mom asked me to take some pictures of you today. What do you think?" he asked.

Think? I had no idea what to think, except that he must be a Scientologist and my parents must know him somehow.

It was hot sitting in the sun, sitting leg to leg. I felt warm. My cheeks felt like they were starting to turn pink from the heat and the closeness of this man. My freckled nose began to perspire, small miniscule beads of sweat forming on my forehead, too. How long will we sit here? I wondered.

John reached down and unbuckled the gold-colored locks on his black briefcase. Then he reached inside and extracted a black leather folder that contained his portfolio of pictures, housed inside plastic sleeves, and bound to the black binding of the folder.

As he opened the portfolio and began to show me his pictures, he narrated the story of each girl.

"This is Jenny. I took this picture at her apartment. She wants to be an actress and she just started her auditing and training at Celebrity Centre. A beautiful girl."

I looked at the photograph. She was beautiful. Long strawberry-blonde hair. Pretty hazel eyes and a sweet, sultry smile. Her nude body was slightly draped by a burgundy red sheet or blanket. Her bare buttocks, smooth, round, and inviting reminded me of pictures I had snuck a peek at in daddy's *Playboy* magazines.

One of her breasts peeked out from the covering to reveal a light-brown areola and pert, pink nipple.

Staring at the glossy photographs, my mind raced. Did he expect me to take off my clothes? Where? What about mommy and my little brother? If we went into our apartment, they would be there. Would he take me to his apartment or studio? And hadn't he noticed, I didn't look anything like this incredibly-photogenic beauty.

Underneath my yellow homemade dress, my tiny buds of breasts had just started to manifest themselves, ever so slightly. I couldn't even boast an areola or a nipple at this stage in my physical development. I was a child. I felt embarrassed, and then angry. Why did mommy let him come over here and show me these pictures? What was she thinking?

"So," he said, as he completely covered my small kneecap with his hand. It was larger than daddy's hands and softer, covered with a white dusting of hair. His nails were short and groomed. "Where should we take your picture?"

He closed the portfolio and put it back into his black briefcase, clicking the gold locks shut. Jenny was trapped inside.

I looked down at the cement and said nothing.

"Well, let's look around here. What about that potted palm over there?" he suggested. "The light might be best there."

He stood up and walked over to the plastic tree that sat on the edge of the pool patio. The large plastic palm leaves were dirty, covered in dust and grime from Los Angeles air pollution.

I followed him to the tree, glancing down at the black briefcase.

As I walked behind him, I wondered. Will anyone ever take pictures of me like the ones that Jenny took? Will I ever look like Jenny? Probably, when I'm thirteen years old, I thought.

John directed me to stand in front of the tree as he poised his camera to his eye. My yellow sleeved arms hung down by my sides as I stood slouched in front of the dirty palm tree. He moved the camera away from his eye and scowled. Of course, I thought, I don't look like Jenny!

The look of annoyance on his face reminded me of mommy's expression when I didn't understand something or when I didn't do something right the very first time that she told me.

"Pamela," she would say, "not like that. I showed you once. Why can't you do it right?"

Exasperated, she would look at me, take a long drag on her cigarette, and then stare off into the distance, as if pondering my inadequacies.

As I posed next to the potted palm, mommy came out and brought me a fake light green pear from the bowl of wax fruit that sat on our kitchen table in the apartment. She and John thought I should hold it. Holding the black camera to his eye, he told me to look at him, but not to smile. He looked through the small opening where he could see me and clicked the button on top. I watched like a frozen statue as he shot the roll of film.

Thankfully, after snapping numerous pictures of me, the photo shoot ended and John left without even saying goodbye to mommy. Returning to our apartment, I saw her in the kitchen. I slipped past her and walked to the bathroom to take off the yellow dress. Gazing in the mirror again, I scornfully looked at my reflection, carefully studying my bare, flat chest and round tummy. I couldn't wait to turn thirteen. You will be pretty like Jenny then, I told myself.

When John brought the prints to show mommy, probably about a week or two later, she called me over from where I was playing outside to take a look at them. The three of us, me, mommy and John, sat down on the chaise lounge chairs that lined the perimeter of the pool. I was excited to see if he had been able to transform me into a beautiful model, like Jenny, the girl he'd shown me, except clothed.

Mommy was clearly disappointed as she looked through the color photographs. She commented that my hair was still wet from swimming and that I wasn't smiling. Listening to her, my head filled with questions. Had she expected the pictures to look different? She was present when they were taken. Didn't she remember that she had dragged me out of the pool to take them?

Coolly, John responded, "Well, yes, but look at her eyes and her serene expression," pointing to one of the photographs. "Pam's beauty is captured here."

My beauty! What is he talking about? I thought. I'm twelve years old with wet hair and freckles, dressed in a handmade dress, holding a plastic piece of fruit next to an ugly potted palm. I looked at mommy to see her reaction.

She looked over at me and said, "The dress is very pretty. I'm glad I kept the sleeves on the dress sheer. The pattern called for them to be sown out of the same material as the bodice, but I thought the sheer sleeves would look better."

I watched as the corners of John's mouth turned up ever so slightly. A wry smile appeared on his face.

"I agree," he coolly replied. "What do you think about me coming back and taking some more photos of Pam? Perhaps in her bathing suit? I like the way her damp hair frames her face."

Mommy momentarily pondered his request. Then she stood up. Holding the folder of photographs, she turned to John and said, "Let me think about it. I want to show these to Paul."

And that was that. John got up from the chaise lounge. Standing next to me, he looked down at me and winked, then he told me that he looked forward to seeing me again.

Mommy never asked John to take more pictures and, perhaps intentionally, she never framed them. They remained in the same folder that he gave her that day, inside one of my childhood photo albums of annual school pictures. Did she pay him to photograph me? Did he try to convince her to let him take more photographs? Probably. But thankfully, I never saw him again.

But it would not be surprising to learn that he continued taking pictures of young girls and women, grooming them for a portfolio that could and would be sold to cover the cost of his auditing and training. Quite a scam. But Scientology preyed on the innocent and the trusting, manipulating its members through deception and lies. John. What an appropriate name. He was, after all, a John of sorts.

⌖

MOMMY'S PSYCHOSIS

By the end of that summer, I learned mommy suffered from psychosis: periodic mental states of mind which included delusions, hallucinations, and a loss of reality.

Her Scientology auditing sessions had stirred up old traumas and troubling life events, in addition to alleged memories and tales from past lives. Delving deeper and deeper into her darkest thoughts while going through the "Operating Thetan" or OT Levels,, auditing that purportedly increased one's abilities to manipulate matter, space, and time, greatly contributed to her madness.

It seemed that, for her, trying to get better through Scientology was like drinking a powerful elixir that she thought could eliminate something bad, something inside her mind that was causing her distress and harm. Yet the irony was that the more she immersed herself in Scientology, the sicker she became.

Mommy's voice was loud and audible. Her singing sounded like a mixture of talking and chanting. Not a song, but more like words strung together in a sort of singsong fashion. My little brother looked at me, bewildered and afraid when he heard her.

I grabbed his hand and dragged him toward the apartment kitchen. Our apartment was always very dark. Mommy kept the ugly brownish green curtains closed. If opened, they would have revealed a sliding glass door that led to the patio area that surrounded the pool on the first floor of our apartment building.

In the kitchen, I told my little brother to sit down at the table and I would make him some lunch.

He protested, "I want to watch cartoons instead."

"You can watch cartoons after lunch," I replied, speaking in a very authoritarian big sister voice to my little brother who was three-and-a-half years younger. We were clearly children fending for ourselves.

As he sat down dejectedly at the small kitchen table, he looked at me sadly and asked, "Can you make me a peanut butter and jelly sandwich? With lots of jelly. Like mommy makes it."

Of course, I thought. Just the way our crazy mommy, who could be heard loudly ranting naked in the bathroom, makes it.

For some reason, probably because the apartment manager, who lived next door to us, called him, daddy came home from work early.

As he opened the front door of the apartment, quickly shutting it behind him, he asked, "Where's your mom?"

I glanced down at my little brother who looked like he might burst into tears. Then I looked directly at daddy. Feeling very brave, I said, "She's taking a shower."

He looked at me quizzically. Mommy never took showers. She always took a bath. Daddy knew this. Looking past me, he walked toward the bathroom, firmly turned the doorknob to the bathroom door, and opened it. The water had stopped and mommy could be heard softly mumbling to herself. Daddy quickly shut the door behind him.

I couldn't hear what they were saying, but the sound of muffled conversation emanated from under the closed door, seeping out through the crack where the door and the linoleum floor met, like a toxic, colorless, and odorless gas.

As I tiptoed toward the closed door to try to listen, my little brother started to follow me.

"Wait for me," he whined.

"Shhh!" I put my finger to my lips and waved him back with my hand.

He looked dejected. Tears started to roll down his chubby pink cheeks.

Before I turned around to comfort him, I heard daddy's voice. Firm, but not angry, just direct: "Gloria, it's time to get out of the shower."

I could hear mommy sobbing on the other side of the door. I stood still, listening intently to see if she was going to yell at daddy, but she didn't. It was quiet. Her episode had ended. I turned toward my little brother and motioned for him to go back to the kitchen.

He smiled as we walked back to his peanut butter and grape jelly lunch. He was happy.

Daddy managed to get mommy out of the shower and into the bedroom. I could hear their footsteps from the kitchen. Out of the corner of my eye, I saw mommy holding onto daddy's arm. She was leaning against him, a thin white towel loosely wrapped around her. She held it up against her chest with one hand as they walked slowly toward the bedroom door.

It looked like they were moving in slow motion. For a split second, I wondered if I was dreaming, or if mommy and daddy were really moving so slowly.

"Paul," she quietly sobbed.

Daddy said nothing as he guided her toward the bedroom, holding onto mommy's skinny bare elbow. Her sobs had stopped. Just sniffles, like a small child after they've stopped having a tantrum. He followed her into the bedroom and closed the door behind them.

Alone in the kitchen with my little brother, I took charge and told him we were going outside to play.

At first, he balked, "No, I'm still eating."

"I'll give you two Oreos for dessert," I bribed.

"Mommy lets me have four cookies," he reminded me.

I sighed. "All right. I'll give you four Oreos. Then we're going outside to play by the pool."

I handed him the blue-and-white plastic package of cookies. He reached in and took a handful. I was too annoyed to discipline him, so I pretended that I didn't see how many cookies were in his hand. I put the package back in the cupboard and we headed outside.

As I opened the door of our apartment, I saw our landlady, Mrs. LaPierre. She stood in front of the closed screen door to her apartment with her son, Mark. Gazing intently at us with a look of disgust, she watched as my little brother and I walked out of our apartment.

I closed the door quickly behind us and kept my eyes down,

only looking at the cement as we walked. Grabbing my little brother's empty hand, the one without the cookies, passed them as I led him toward the patio that surrounded the pool.

The LaPierres' apartment door was open, allowing the little breeze that existed to enter through the specially-installed screen door. It was a hot summer day in L.A., the temperature outside probably in the mid-eighties. Mrs. LaPierre's hand rested on the screen door handle as if she was just getting ready to open it and go inside.

In a curt, superior tone of voice, she asked, "Where is your mother?" Even though she spoke in English, her French-Canadian accent was thick.

I turned to look at her. "She's resting," I responded meekly, talking mostly to the cement.

My simple response immediately set her off. She practically spit at me and my little brother as she began to rant loudly in French, her native language. Mark and his parents were French-Canadian from Quebec who had moved to California when he was little. Mark told me this one day while we were outside playing.

"We are Quebecois," he proudly stated.

I had no idea what that meant. Was it another religion, like Scientology? I thought.

"We're from Quebec," he added, full of Canadian pride.

"Where's Quebec?" I asked.

With an audible sigh, he rolled his eyes, put his hands on his slender hips, and replied, "Canada, of course." As if his declaration clearly defined why both he and his mother were superior to us.

Not sure where to go, or what to do next, I took my little brother's hand and turned to walk back to our apartment. I listened for a moment outside the door, but I didn't hear anything. It was quiet.

Slowly, I turned the doorknob and led my little brother back inside. We walked into the living room and I turned on the TV, moving the dial until I found a cartoon that I knew he liked. We both sat down cross-legged on the ugly, rough shag carpeting.

Mommy's sobs could be heard over the sound of the cartoon characters that flashed across the TV screen, while loud commercials for soap detergent drowned out the sound of her cries. While my little brother was engrossed in his favorite cartoon, I got up and walked to mommy's bedroom door, just past the bathroom. The door was slightly ajar. I peeked inside.

Through the small opening, I saw her. She was lying on the bed in a fetal position, curled up in a ball like a baby. Holding her knees with her hands, she rocked back and forth. The towel daddy had used to cover her when she came out of the shower had fallen on the floor. She was naked.

Her package of opened cigarettes sat on the nightstand next to her bed, a black ashtray and a pack of matches sat next to them. The trifecta. They were her salve and her comfort. I watched her as she mumbled softly to herself between sobs. Her words were unintelligible.

Then I realized daddy was no longer in the apartment. He'd left mommy alone to come out of her psychotic stupor by herself. I wondered if he'd gone back to work. I closed the bedroom door, careful to not make a sound as I silently walked back to the living room.

My little brother was still watching cartoons, immersed in the antics and bravery of superheroes. I sat back down next to him and wondered what would happen to mommy. Her anger and her fits of rage toward daddy were familiar, but this was not. I was frightened by her frailty, and by what appeared to be a sudden lapse from us and from reality.

VISITING MOMMY

Soon after the shower incident, mommy was taken to a Scientology "safe house" so Scientologists could keep a closer eye on her. It was easier to "control" her behavior under Scientology's twenty-four-hour watch than to wait for another psychotic episode" to happen. Silencing reports of Scientologists' crazy behavior was essential. "Only report 'wins'" was definitely Scientology's mantra.

During the early 1970s, L. Ron Hubbard wrote several bulletins that outlined how to handle Scientologists who were exhibiting psychoses. The bulletins were mostly Hubbard's instructions on what the auditor should do, and the auditor reporting back what happened when the instructions were followed.

The key to helping someone in mental distress, Hubbard theorized, was to put them in isolation and remove outside stimuli—

to give them the silent treatment—until they calmed down and then were "sessionable" and could undergo a complex regimen of auditing.

We visited mommy once while she was in the "safe house," which was really just an apartment in a small complex called the Lanai. Many Scientologists who worked at the Advanced Organization of Los Angeles lived there. It wasn't far from our own apartment building, maybe a ten-minute drive.

Daddy picked me up from our apartment after school and we drove in silence the entire way there. After parking in front of the apartment complex, we walked through a small concrete courtyard surrounded by small potted palms similar to our own apartment building, only smaller.

The Scientologist who had been assigned to be mommy's "caretaker" opened the door when daddy knocked, and let us into the small apartment. Then she led us from the front door to a bedroom where mommy was being held.

When we walked into the bedroom, I saw her. She was sitting up in a small twin bed. Her hair was unkept and she didn't have any make-up on. Her bony shoulders protruded from underneath a thin cotton nightgown. The rest of her body, except for her long, skinny arms, was covered with a thin white sheet. It was late afternoon, but she looked like she'd just woken up.

"Gloria, your husband and daughter are here to see you," her caretaker casually stated as she turned and walked out of the room, leaving the bedroom door open.

My parents' eyes locked as we entered the room. Mommy's gaze was steady. She didn't smile, but she also didn't look sad.

The room was strangely quiet. There were no displays of affection for either one of us. No hugs or kisses. But mommy didn't seem surprised to see us, as if it was normal for her to be there and for us to visit her.

Daddy and I stood at the foot of the bed looking at mommy, waiting for our next direction from the caretaker, who reentered the bedroom, walked over to the side of the bed, and stood next to mommy.

Looking directly at daddy, she confidently reported on mommy's progress.

"Gloria's been resting. She's taking the Cal Mag (a combination of calcium and magnesium supplements, prescribed by LRH as part of the regime for handling psychosis) and she's eating."

He nodded and replied, "Good."

Then, in a firm tone the caretaker turned toward mommy and asked, "Gloria, do you want to talk to Paul or Pam?"

Mommy looked up at her. She was silent, as if pondering the question or waiting for further directions.

Finally, after a long pause, she matter-of-factly stated, "Sure."

The caretaker nodded at daddy as she walked out of the bedroom again.

"Hi, Gloria. Pam and I came to visit you," daddy spoke slower than normal, as if he was talking to a young child or perhaps someone who couldn't comprehend the language he was using.

Mommy looked up at him, unreactive to his words; she continued to stare at him intently, as if she was pondering what he'd just said. I didn't know what to think of this new behavior, considering the last few times that I'd seen mommy she was ranting naked in the shower, crying uncontrollably, or spaced out in our apartment. I wondered. Was she okay? Could she understand him?

Finally, mommy replied, and stated in an ever so recognizable sarcastic tone of voice, "Yes. I can see that."

Upon hearing her response, the corners of daddy's mouth turned up for just a second, as if he might break into a smile, but he quickly pulled his lips together, keeping his mouth closed. Then, he turned and looked down at me, standing next to him, quietly taking in this new family scene.

I hoped that he would say we were going to leave. But instead, he gave me a directive, "Pam, why don't you tell your mom about school."

School! I thought. I don't want to talk about school and I'm almost positive mommy doesn't want to hear about school. I wasn't even sure she wanted us near her.

Embarrassed, I felt myself blush as I looked at mommy's face. She stared at me. Almost like a dare. Would I talk to her, like daddy had directed me to do? With both of my parents staring at me, I hesitated. Not knowing what else to say, I began telling her about a book that I was reading at school.

Immediately, I could tell by mommy's expression and by her body language that I'd chosen the wrong thing to say. Her face twisted into a grimace, as if I'd uttered bad words or there was a bad smell in the room. She stiffened her arms and began rubbing the sheet between her fingers as if she wanted to get rid of something that was on her hands.

The caretaker, who had moved to the back of the room, next to the bedroom door, stepped forward and looked directly at mommy and asked,

"Gloria, are you ready for your family to leave?" Mommy continued to rub her fingers between the folds of the sheet that covered her. As she moved her hand rhythmically, she looked at me and spoke. Her words felt like daggers, sharp and hurtful as they struck me. "Pamela, I don't care what you are reading. I'm not feeling well. I don't want to talk about what you're reading. I need to rest and get better."

Holding back tears, I put my head down and looked at the dirty brown shag carpet under my feet. Why did I bother to talk to her? I thought.

As soon as mommy finished talking, the caretaker moved toward daddy and whispered something to him under her breath.

Daddy nodded, shifting his weight from one foot to the other, and stated matter-of-factly, "It's time to go, Pam."

Daddy and I drove back to our apartment in silence.

• • •

Even after mommy was "released" and allowed to come back to our apartment, she continued to exhibit incoherent rants that were difficult to understand, almost as though she was speaking another language. She would pace back and forth in the living room, mumbling and chain-smoking packages of Kool cigarettes for what seemed like hours.

She also suffered from crying binges that lasted for days. Holed up in her bedroom, she wouldn't come out except to use the bathroom and to make herself cups of coffee. I could hear her wailing and thrashing in her bed, then softly sobbing as she wiped her eyes and walked to the bathroom, glancing at me and my little brother playing in our bedroom as she passed by.

After using the bathroom, or visiting the kitchen for more coffee, she would peek in and say, "Hi, kids. You know I love you. I just need to rest a little bit more."

As a Scientologist, due to her "aberrant" or unruly behavior, she had become somewhat of a liability, mostly because she wasn't progressing up the "Bridge to Total Freedom" as cleanly and neatly as her auditors and case supervisor had planned. She'd become difficult. Although she did what she was told to do by the Scientologists who visited our apartment after she was "released," it seemed like she was allowed only a small degree of free will.

It was also apparent that her agoraphobia, an anxiety disorder in which you fear and avoid places or situations that might cause you to panic or feel trapped, had grown exceedingly worse.

Many years earlier, on the night before her wedding, she experienced her first panic attack. Mommy talked about it often, as if she was constantly reliving the event in the present. Although I dreaded hearing about it, she never seemed to tire of telling me about it, adding new details and embellishments with each retelling. It became part of her repertoire.

Her story always started with the night before her wedding day. She was sitting on the quilt-covered twin bed in daddy's childhood bedroom. His mother had insisted that she stay the night there. It made sense. The reception was going to be held in daddy's childhood home. They were only going to the justice of the peace in town to get married. She would be closer than all the way in Bethel, where she still lived with her parents.

Her wedding dress hung in the closet. A simple white dress that she'd bought off the rack at the local department store. Her own mother could have made it, but she didn't want that. This was not the wedding she'd imagined!

It wasn't even a simple wedding with a guest list of a few friends. Only relatives would be present. She really couldn't invite her sorority sisters. Not only was that too expensive, but realistically, too embarrassing. She'd left the University of Kansas after her second year because she couldn't afford the tuition. Her sorority sisters had all graduated and married fraternity brothers. Sitting on the bed, she contemplated why she'd even agreed to marry daddy.

Panic enveloped her like a vice around her chest. She felt as if she couldn't breathe, as if something or someone had taken hold of her lungs and squeezed them shut. Sitting on the bed, she looked around the room; her breathing became shallow. She felt trapped. Why was the room so small? She looked at the white wooden-framed window above the bed. It was closed. Kansas in June. Hot and humid. The closed window was covered by sheer, flowered curtains.

Standing up, she felt lightheaded from the heat and too little dinner. She steadied herself by clutching the brown, maple headboard. With her right hand, she reached to pull back the yellow-and-pink-flowered curtains. The sky was almost black with a lonely bluish-tinted three-quarter moon.

Then, building up to the climax, she told me how she'd thought about opening the window and quietly leaving, without daddy or his mother knowing. She imagined opening the window and gingerly climbing out so as not to make any detectable noise. The curtains would be left blowing wistfully in the warm evening air, slightly scented by the pink and white roses that grew beneath the window.

She could almost feel her bare feet touch the soft grass below. The story always ended dramatically as she described snagging her yellow cotton summer dress on the rosebush, yanking it free, slightly tearing the pale, yellow hem and pricking her finger as she turned and ran.

But, in comparison, the fear and panic that she now experienced was so intense that she was unable to leave our apartment building. She would venture out to the pool area or to a fellow Scientologist's apartment, who lived in the same complex. But going to the store caused her so much anxiety that she sent my little brother or me to the local liquor store to purchase her cigarettes as well as snacks, milk, bread, and other necessities.

As young kids, we felt somewhat grown-up and important when mommy handed us money to go buy these "essentials" across the street. We even established an interesting rapport with the liquor store owner, who never seemed to question us as he put mommy's carton of cigarettes along with our food items in a brown paper bag. Yet he surely knew that he was breaking the law by selling cigarettes to minors.

LIFE IN L.A.,
EARTHQUAKES & DISNEYLAND,
CIRCA 1970-1971

We were still living on Bonnie Brae Avenue when one eventful morning, at six am, on February 9, 1971, my little brother and I woke up to a shaking scene. The bedside lamp that sat on the table between us violently started rocking back and forth. I watched as my little brother bounced up and down in his twin bed just a few feet away. Jolted awake by the movement, he started crying and tried to get out of his bed to come into mine.

"Pam, I'm scared. What is it? Let me get in your bed," he whined frantically.

"No! Don't get out of bed," I yelled at him, afraid that the wobbling lamp might fall on him.

He whimpered under his covers as he rode the last of the jolts with his head buried under a pillow.

After what seemed to be minutes, but was actually only a

documented twelve seconds, I watched the lamp begin to settle down. Miraculously, it never fell over. Abruptly, our beds stopped shaking and the earthquake was over. Just like that.

As if it were synchronized the phone, that sat next to the lamp on the bedside table in our room began to ring. Startled, I stared at it, then picked up the black receiver after the second ring.

I heard daddy's voice on the other end.

"Hi Pam, did you feel the earthquake?"

Literally shaken and feeling very frightened, I thought, Of course I did! How could I not feel it?! But not wanting to let daddy know my true level of fear, I lied and told him, "Yes. We were a little scared."

His response pretty much summed up his capacity for empathy, compassion, and fatherly concern. "Yeah, it was pretty strong out here. I could feel it even while I was driving. I just got to work and wanted to see if you felt it there. All right. See you tonight."

I heard the click on the other end as he hung up. Lowering the phone away from my right ear, I frowned at the black object in my hand as I placed it back on its base.

My little brother, bare feet hanging down over the side of his bed, clad in his blue Superman pajama bottoms and top emblazoned with a red "S," asked me if daddy was coming home.

Secretly, I wished we had the kind of daddy that would come home and comfort us.

But in my best pretend grown-up twelve-year-old voice, I said, "No, he's at work. It was an earthquake. We need to get up and get ready for school."

Following our usual morning routine, we both got dressed,

fixed ourselves bowls of cereal, doused in milk, and watched cartoons before we headed out of the apartment. We seldom watched the local news, preferring cartoons to the boring weather report and daily depressing news reports of the Vietnam War. It never entered my mind to turn the channel and listen for any earthquake updates.

After closing the apartment door, I locked it with the key I kept on a piece of yarn attached to my brown suede-fringed purse. We were "latchkey kids," and had learned quickly how to let ourselves in and out of our apartment without the assistance of an adult.

As we turned to enter the patio courtyard, I saw Mrs. LaPierre, standing in her open doorway. Mark stood next to her. They looked like carbon copies of each other. Hands on their hips. Matching sour, downturned scowls, almost smirks, on their faces.

She watched me and my little brother as we started to walk. Her stare was steady, and the disgusted look on her face matched the cruel tone of her voice.

In her thick, French-Canadian accent, laced with venom, she asked, "Where are you going?"

I looked at her somewhat incredulously, as it seemed perfectly obvious to me that we were going to school just like we did every morning. I glanced over at Mark before answering.

He was not an ally in this conversation. His stance, his gaze, and his words were just as accusatory.

"Well?" he asked, hands still firmly planted on his slender hips.

I looked at Mark first, and then his mother, as I answered meekly, "To school."

They both looked at us pathetically, then smiled at each other knowingly. In unison, they began to chuckle loudly, sounding like cackling hens, or chortling pigs. I stood there, holding my little brother's hand as their laughter began to subside, thinking to myself, now, what?

Then Mark looked right at me and began speaking, in a "know-it-all" tone of voice, "There isn't any school today. The schools are closed because of the earthquake. Just go back into your apartment."

As Mark and his mother turned and went back into their apartment next-door, I saw Mark glance at me over his shoulder. In spite of his mother's disapproving stare, his look spoke volumes, especially his eyes, which I believed were trying to tell me, "I'm sorry. You must be scared. I can't help you now, but maybe later."

Maybe, I thought, as my little brother and I walked back to our apartment. I quickly unlocked the door with my key, shut it behind me, and turned the deadbolt lock inside. We were prisoners inside our apartment once again. Little did I know that my little brother and I would feel numerous aftershocks throughout the day and into the weeks that followed from the magnitude 6.6 Sylmar earthquake.

As I turned the TV back on and found my little brother's favorite cartoon show, I decided, rather confidently, that earthquakes didn't seem quite as scary as hurricanes. At least they didn't last as long and your house didn't flood.

But still cautious, and not sure if we would feel more shaking, I stayed close to my little brother in the living room, watching cartoons with him. Sitting side by side on the dirty carpet in front of the TV, we watched Batman and Robin's antics play out on the screen in front of us. "Bam!", "Pow!", and "Off to the Batmobile!" My little brother was entertained while I waited for the next aftershock.

That afternoon, I did walk out of the apartment a few times, hoping Mark might be outside. But he wasn't. I felt alone and scared. Mommy had temporarily returned to the Scientology "safe house," and daddy was at work. While I waited for more aftershocks, I sat next to my little brother, who was pretty good at playing by and entertaining himself, and read one of his Archie Comics books.

Daddy didn't come home until later that evening. Driving from the Lockheed Aircraft facility in Palmdale, where he worked, in the late afternoon traffic, to our apartment in L.A., was at least a two-hour journey. With both of our parents absent, we fended for ourselves.

• • •

Sadly, when mommy returned from the Scientology "safe house," her agoraphobia, instead of dissipating, became increasingly worse and debilitating, rendering her unable to enjoy life or spend time with us outside of the apartment. Did daddy know about the panic and terror that mommy felt whenever she tried to leave the house? It's hard to imagine that he didn't.

One day, when daddy came home from work, he told us that his office was handing out Disneyland passes for Lockheed Family Night. My little brother and I were excited! We'd never been to Disneyland. But when he told mommy about the tickets, she didn't seem particularly happy.

Daddy even tried to coax her into joining us by saying, "Come on, Gloria. It'll be fun. The tickets are free."

Sitting at the dining room table, smoking a cigarette, mommy looked at daddy and replied, "No, I don't think so. You and the kids go."

"C'mon, Gloria. Why not? What are you going to do if you stay here? You've got to leave the apartment sometime," daddy persisted.

Mommy looked up at daddy, almost pleadingly, and replied, "Paul, you know I can't go. Don't keep badgering me, please."

Daddy grinned at mommy and said, "Okay. Suit yourself," and that was the end of the conversation.

In 1971, Disneyland D and E tickets were the highlight of a purchased ticket book. You only got a few and you knew to spend them wisely. The Matterhorn was an E ticket ride. Fast and fun! But that evening, Disneyland was closed to outsiders, only friends and family of Lockheed employees allowed. We could walk from ride to ride without worrying about tickets or how to best use them. Basically, Disneyland was free. Lines were short, and the night air was magical.

The dark, clear sky, lit up by the lights on Main Street, greeted us as we entered. Walking into Fantasyland, we could hear the sound of the snowstorm and the howling wind in Matterhorn Mountain. Listening to the sound of the fake wind, we stood in line, waiting for a Matterhorn bobsled that would transport us on the rails that zoomed around the snowy mountain. After boarding our bobsled, my little brother whimpered behind me as I sat next to daddy, terrified but silent.

Daddy grinned and chuckled, almost sinisterly, as we jerked along the clacking rails and whooshed down the mountain. Then, as quickly as it began, the ride was over. Our fiberglass bobsled came to a sudden stop at the bottom of the mountain where it rested next to a brown Alpine-decorated wooden chalet.

As daddy climbed out of the bobsled, he shouted, "Let's go get on the Teacups!"

My little brother responded, "I don't want to go. I feel sick."

These were my sentiments exactly. But I knew very well that our feelings would be overruled. As we clamored into a pink teacup, I looked up at the brightly-colored hanging lanterns swaying in the breeze.

The cups began to move across the floor of the lit pavilion. Daddy firmly grabbed the wheel in the middle of the teacup. With both hands, he began to turn it. The teacup spun, faster and faster, as it danced around the other teacups. Children laughed and screamed, their heads thrown back, mouths open, eyes wide.

My little brother and I sat in silence as daddy's strong grip kept turning the metal wheel. Our teacup was going so fast! I was afraid it might spin right off its base. I looked straight ahead, trying to anchor myself and not throw up. But out of the corner of my eye, I quickly glimpsed at daddy's face. His grin was wide, his eyes wild with glee behind his black-framed glasses.

In that split second, I hated him. I hated him the way I believed mommy hated him. It was a deep hate that had to be silenced and sequestered or else it might consume me. It was the kind of hate that hurt.

Back home, mommy had waited up for us. As daddy opened the

door and we entered the apartment, she looked at us, cigarette in hand, and asked, "So, how was Disneyland?"

"Great!" daddy and I both replied.

"It was all right," my little brother muttered. "I wish you'd come with us."

Defiance, pity, and my mother's smoke filled the room.

Disneyland became a ying and yang childhood experience for me, where joy and laughter met fear and dread.

ANOTHER MOVE

We moved to our new apartment on Lafayette Park Place just before I started junior high school. Such a grand street name. It reminded me of high-end property names in one of my favorite games, Monopoly.

But although it wasn't very grand, the move was definitely a step up, as it was in a somewhat less-seedy part of Los Angeles, situated near Rampart Boulevard and Temple Street. Next to our apartment building, rows of somewhat-new apartment complexes, similar to ours, stretched down the long block.

On moving day, before the furniture arrived, daddy did something I'd never seen him do before. He practiced walking back and forth, from wall to wall, in the empty carpeted living room of our new apartment. Putting his arms out in front of him for balance, he walked back and forth, touching the blank white wall on the other side, or sometimes falling into the wall with his shoulder. Then he'd rest there for a minute and start up again, a determined, pained grimace on his face.

Each time he started, I heard him mumble, "Walk to that wall."

When he arrived at the other side, I heard him say, "Thank you."

As he stood in front of the wall, or rested against it, he mumbled to himself, "Touch that wall."

Reaching out to touch the wall with his hand, he ended by saying, "Thank you."

When I asked daddy what he was doing, he told me he was following Scientology commands that were part of a Communication Course drill. It didn't make any sense to me, and it was hard watching daddy as he walked, stumbled, and eventually fell.

I even tried to stop him, "Daddy, stop! You're going to fall!"

Stubbornly, he ignored my pleas and continued the drill. Finally, after about ten or fifteen laps, he collapsed on the floor and sat on the green shag carpet, catching his breath and staring at his legs.

He sat on the floor with his hands firmly planted at his sides, trying to hoist himself back up. But his legs had given out. He couldn't will them to bend or stand. Looking over at me, he held out his hand for me to grab. I walked over and looked down at his crumpled legs resting on the carpet.

At twelve years old, I was a small child, not tiny but certainly not tall for my age. I couldn't lift him or even attempt to lift his two-hundred-fifty-pound body, especially when he had no strength in his legs. I felt sorry for him. But I was also resentful and angry.

Why do I have to help him up? I thought. Where's mommy? Why isn't she here? This was my constant lament.

Determined, daddy turned over, and put all his weight on his knees. As he grabbed the wooden bar countertop adjacent to the kitchen, he hoisted himself up to a standing position. His grunts and groans filled the empty apartment as I helplessly watched.

Waiting for him to catch his breath, and hopefully regain his strength, I looked around the new apartment. As I scanned the living room and kitchen, I realized the décor and color scheme somewhat resembled our home in Slidell, including the green shag carpeting with gold accent threads, and the olive green appliances in the kitchen.

But there was also an interesting addition, a faux Greco-Roman-style wallpaper mural on one wall that depicted columns and urns surrounded by a Mediterranean-style scene. I thought it was kind of funny that this mural of the Mediterranean Sea and places we'd sailed by on the *Royal Scotman* years earlier now graced our new apartment.

Although mostly empty at first, not long after we moved in, mommy went on a spending spree and proceeded to buy all of the Ethan Allen furniture that daddy had sold, or gotten rid of in Louisiana, due to the foreclosure. It seemed very important to her to recreate the life she'd left, and then lost, or at least it appeared that way to me.

• • •

I was pretty sure that our move to the new apartment was also, partly, so my little brother could attend a better school, but I also started to think that our move across town might have something to do with mommy, and of course, Scientology.

Since arriving in Los Angeles, mommy had been receiving auditing and training at AOLA. This was also the Org that "handled" her first psychotic episode, and put her in a "safe house."

But before we moved, I heard mommy and daddy talking about a different Org called the American Saint Hill Organization. I'm fairly certain our move was so mommy would be closer to ASHO, which was just a few blocks up the street. The Org was easily within walking distance. But at first, mommy rarely walked there or even went outside because she was still mostly housebound due to her agoraphobia.

I began to wonder if mommy's "case" was too difficult for AOLA, and that was why we were moving, so she could get different, or better, training and auditing. But I really didn't understand how Scientology Orgs worked or the severity of mommy's agoraphobia.

Yet it wasn't long before mommy did start going to ASHO. One afternoon, I heard her talking to daddy about it. They also talked about overts and omissions, which I'd heard them talk about before. But this time, the conversation didn't seem to upset mommy, at least not the part I heard.

I'd gone into the kitchen to see what mommy was making for dinner. She was sitting at the kitchen table, smoking a cigarette, and daddy was sitting across from her. An open Scientology book lay on the table in front of him. But I couldn't see the cover, so I wasn't sure which one he was reading.

As I peeked at the pot on the stove, I heard daddy read out loud to mommy, "According to LRH, there is a direct ratio between the health and ability of the person and his willingness to accept responsibility."

I waited for mommy to say something. She usually didn't like it when daddy quoted Scientology doctrine. I was surprised to see her just listening and nodding her head.

Then daddy reminded mommy, "Gloria, Scientology can only work when your overts and omissions are handled."

I knew this meant that mommy needed to admit to a Scientology auditor anything bad she'd done or even thought about doing.

Mommy looked at daddy, but she didn't react. She just sat there, looking sad, smoking her cigarette in silence. As I left the kitchen, neither mommy nor daddy seemed to even notice me.

Several days later, while looking for a pad of paper to write on, I found a list of "confessions" on several pieces of yellow legal notepad paper. The list was written in blue ink, in mommy's handwriting.

Using Scientology terminology, mommy's list included how she'd "enterbulated daddy," which meant she'd upset him. She also wrote that she'd "third partied," meaning she'd interfered with something. Mommy's list was long, and even included how she'd "nattered," which meant complained, about the Scientology Orgs.

Mommy's list began:

> *I enturbulated Paul tonight. I enturbulated him.*
> *I made nothing of his (life). I third partied.*
> *I have denied myself medical attention.*
> *I've nattered to Paul about AOLA and staff members.*
> *I've acted as a victim. I carried on last night making Paul guilty.*
> *I've withheld information on my case.*
> *I've expected Paul to be responsible for me and my case.*

As I read more, I learned mommy felt badly about not taking my little brother and I to the doctor, and for missing our school conferences.

> *I've refused to take responsibility for myself and my children.*
> *I didn't take them to the doctor for stitches.*
> *I didn't attend their conferences at school.*

Was mommy admitting that she'd neglected me and my little brother? I didn't think she even cared. As I continued reading, I couldn't believe she'd done all the things she listed, to us, to Scientology, and to daddy.

> *I gave a Touch Assist incorrectly.*
> *I've had vicious thoughts recently about Ron, AOLA staff members, and Scientology in general.*
> *I've tried to get Paul out of Scientology.*
> *I've tried to push Scientology as being wrong to Paul.*
> *I've tried to get Paul to believe that Scientology is bad.*
> *I've third partied Scientology, Scientologists, and AOLA staff members to Paul.*
> *I've hoped Paul would lose ARC (I've tried to covertly instigate this) with Scientology to get out of it.*
> *I kept Paul away from Scientology during the years after we left the D.C., Org. I have tried to prove Scientology didn't work.*
> *In doing all this, I've made myself get worse and worse and more and more psychotic.*

But most upsetting was what I read next:

> *I've been suppressive to myself, to Paul, to my children,*
>   *and to AOLA staff members.*
> *I lied to Mary Sue, to Scott Leland, my auditor, and to all the*
>   *people on the ship, telling them I was going to Saint Hill*
>   *to do the Briefing Course, but I had no intention of doing*
>   *so. I was just doing it to get away.*
> *I refused by omission Ron's help when on the* Royal Scotman,
>   *aware that he was offering it, and by his being there*
>   *would have been offering to help.*
> *I've blamed Scientology for my misunderstood, rather than be*
>   *responsible for this.*

Shocked by mommy's "confessions," I read the list again. I couldn't understand why mommy wrote that Scientology was bad. And it seemed almost impossible to me that she'd tried to get daddy to leave Scientology. Hadn't we gone to Saint Hill and sailed on the *Royal Scotman* so mommy could get more auditing and training? Didn't mommy leave us in Slidell, and come to California, because of Scientology? Wasn't Scientology the reason we were in California? It didn't make sense.

But I did know that in Scientology, a "Suppressive Person" is anyone who questions, goes against, or influences a Scientologist to try to leave Scientology. Being declared a "Suppressive Person" in Scientology meant you had to "disconnect" from your Scientology friends and family, and never see or speak to them again. I was terrified this might happen to mommy if anyone in Scientology saw her list. I felt confused, but also mad at mommy for all the bad things she'd done. I wondered if daddy had read the list. If he had, I was sure he wasn't going to like it. I wanted to hide the list so daddy wouldn't read it, but instead, I carefully tucked it back under the papers and magazines where I'd found it. It was another secret I needed to keep.

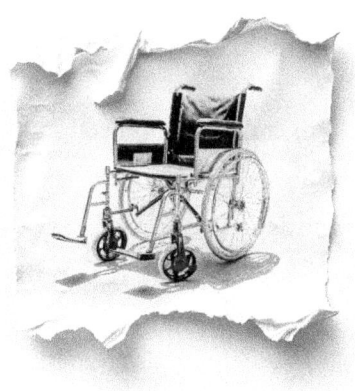

DADDY'S ILLNESS,
CIRCA 1971

D addy's legs began to get worse a few months after we moved into our new apartment. He was still working long hours away from home, and at the end of a long day, he complained of leg pain often. Mommy told him that maybe he needed better shoes for walking. They didn't help, though.

By my thirteenth birthday, daddy's Multiple Sclerosis disease was full-blown. He was in a wheelchair within six months of his diagnosis.

Using a medical dictionary and the *Encyclopedia Britannica*, both books my parents owned, and which sat on bookshelves in our new apartment, mommy researched daddy's symptoms in hopes of figuring out what was wrong with him. She was truly masterful at reading and digging until she found answers. Daddy's medical condition and illness were like a puzzle to her, something to be solved. It was not an emotional pursuit, but more of an academic one.

As she identified his many symptoms, she learned there was a common thread, the loss of vision and the weakness in his legs, which led to the diagnosis of Multiple Sclerosis. Through a spinal tap procedure at the veteran's hospital, the confirmation of his illness led to weeks at the rehabilitation facility, Rancho Los Amigos. When Daddy returned home, he was in a wheelchair.

During that time, because daddy wasn't able to go to work, mommy filled out paperwork for our family to receive veterans' Disability benefits. Daddy qualified because he'd been in the U.S. Navy. We also received food stamps to make sure we were able to eat. In an instant, we plunged from being a middle-class family to, sadly, another poor family in Los Angeles receiving financial assistance in order to survive.

My parents' status as Scientologists also shifted as they no longer had money to pour into auditing and training, which placed them in a different echelon of the Church. Sales stats, along with auditing and training completions, were what mattered most to L. Ron Hubbard and the Scientology Organizations. Sea Org staff who didn't meet their quotas were berated and demeaned by their superiors.

My parents, due to their lack of income, became "nonproducers" in that they didn't contribute financially to Scientology, and their connection to Scientology slowly began to wane. Mommy stopped visiting ASHO, and after being diagnosed, daddy was too ill to take courses or participate in auditing sessions, even if he'd wanted to.

But not long after daddy returned from the rehabilitation facility, although he could no longer walk, and he was wheelchair-bound, he did go back to work for a while. In order to get to work, he decided to purchase a new car, a sporty Dodge Charger, and had it outfitted with hand controls, which his Disability benefits paid for. Even though his legs were paralyzed, his own hands still worked well enough to allow him to use them to control a car, or at least he thought they did.

In his new car, daddy was able to drive to Lockheed, which was more than fifty miles away, in the high desert. The freeways he traveled to the Antelope Valley were not congested, and speeding was a regular practice by those who traveled there, especially in the early morning hours. He loved to drive, especially in his Charger, which was a fast car!

Getting in and out of the car was pretty easy for daddy because his upper body was still strong enough to support his lower body weight. He'd hold onto his wheelchair, slide into the driver's seat, and then me or my little brother would help him collapse his wheelchair and put it in the back seat. At the end of the day, before he left to come home from work, daddy would call us so we could be ready to meet him in the parking garage.

Daddy's drive was almost two hours each way, and he didn't, or couldn't, stop to use the bathroom, so he carried an empty mayonnaise jar, without the label, in his car, urinating in it during his drive. By the end of the day, when he arrived home, the jar was full of bright-yellow pee. One of my tasks was to empty the jar. I began to dread this daily ritual. Mostly because the stench of urine that permeated daddy's car disgusted me.

But this routine worked although it was only temporary. Daddy only worked part-time and for just a few short months before his condition worsened.

· · ·

199

One afternoon, after walking home from my new school, Virgil Junior High School, which was about a mile away, including a brief bus ride on the RTD, Los Angeles's Rapid Transit District transportation system, I stood in the living room of our apartment with mommy.

She was dressed, as usual, in a polyester pantsuit and a white polyester blouse with a pointed collar. The olive green outfit was completed by a matching long green polyester vest, an outfit she'd sewn herself, except for the blouse. Pantsuits were definitely a '70s thing. Mommy owned several of these. They were her 1970s look. Green just happened to be her color of choice that day.

I too was dressed in my own '70s style, hip-hugger denim jeans and a long-sleeved, light-heather-brown knit bodysuit with an attached white collar. My long brown hair, parted perfectly in the middle of my head, hung down the sides of my face, falling past my shoulders to just above my elbows.

At thirteen, I was navigating life with an agoraphobic mommy and a disabled daddy in our new apartment while trying to figure out where I fit in at my school. I was decidedly unsure.

As we stood in the living room, mommy looked over the top of my head, as if she was speaking to the wall behind me, and casually stated, "Your dad wants a Touch Assist."

I looked at her, surprised, disgusted, and then submissive. Then why don't you do it? I thought. But I knew it would be useless to even argue. Daddy had already told her what he wanted. She was just fulfilling his request by offering me up when he asked her to perform the act.

A Touch Assist is a Scientology action for alleviating pain. My parents performed them on both me and my little brother when we were little, usually when we fell down and scraped our knees or elbows. Also sometimes when we had a fever. Did they work? Who knows? They were certainly not medically researched or proven to be effective, except, of course, by Scientologists. But the use of them was part of our Scientology life.

Riding in his electric wheelchair, daddy whirred into the bedroom, my bedroom, the one I shared with my little brother. I silently walked past mommy and into the bedroom. She quickly shut the door behind me. The bedroom had one window that faced the alley behind the apartment building. It was daylight and the sun shone through the closed, uncovered window.

Sitting, waiting for me, daddy was dressed in his white short-sleeved dress shirt and black pants. This was his daily uniform, the one he wore to Lockheed, where he worked as a technical writer. I remember asking him once, or twice, what he did at work. He told me that he wrote manuals about how things worked. How boring, I thought.

Without shoes or socks on, his cracked feet sat lifeless on the silver metal footrests of the wheelchair. They were covered with whitish dry skin that made them look fake, like feet on a wax mannequin. His toenails were yellow and rather long. No one cared to cut them, certainly not mommy, and daddy could no longer groom himself.

Planted on the footrests of his wheelchair, his feet were unmoving, still, and without feeling, as if they were separate entities that had stopped supporting the legs to which they were attached. His pee bag, pungent and fairly full, hung down on one side of his wheelchair. His dirty, dark-black hair was greasy and combed to one side. His hands and arms, covered with the same dark hair, rested on the padded metal arms of the wheelchair. He wore his silver wedding band on his left ring finger, and his Clear Bracelet on his right wrist.

"Feel my finger," I began.

The Touch Assist required a simple command and a polite response, but expected a ridiculous outcome. Relief from pain. At most, the process, as it was called, provided a temporary distraction from the pain and momentarily redirected the person's attention away from the pain. However, true pain, the kind that measures somewhere between six and ten on a scale of one to ten, could not be alleviated, no matter how much touching occurred.

"Feel my finger," I continued as I pushed my finger into daddy's foot and leg, as hard as I could, for what seemed like forever. But sadly, he couldn't even feel the pressure of my efforts. He literally could NOT feel my finger. Daddy's feet and legs were numb. They were paralyzed. The nerve endings had been destroyed by the disease.

Finally, daddy looked down and saw my finger touching his body and responded, "Yes."

"Thank you," I quickly replied, just as I'd been taught. Then I planted my finger on the other side of his leg for another few minutes.

While I waited for his next response, I looked out the window to the alley below us, noting the full garbage cans and the trash that had spilled over onto the gray cement.

I continued pushing my finger into his foot and leg, repeating the command, "Feel my finger."

Daddy stared straight ahead, his body still and unmoving. To each command, he would eventually look down to see my finger, and respond, "Yes."

After about twenty minutes, which again, seemed like forever, daddy told me that he felt better. I'd performed the Touch Assist dutifully, but it was as if I wasn't really present. I felt like I was watching myself, disassociated from him and the feel of his rough, calloused feet, and repulsed by the stench of his urine.

Smiling weakly at him, I got up from where I'd been sitting cross-legged at his feet. Then I walked toward the door, opened it, and went into the kitchen to get something to drink. I heard the whir of daddy's electric wheelchair behind me as he followed me out of the bedroom. Over the next several weeks, I gave daddy many Touch Assists, but the experience didn't get any better for either of us.

· · ·

Several months after daddy came home from the rehabilitation facility, a special bed was sent to our apartment. It arrived one afternoon while I was at school. After walking the six long blocks from the bus stop to our apartment building, I unlocked the apartment door, and there it was on display in the middle of the living room.

Carefully positioned between the couch, the dining room table, and the stereo sat a gray metal hospital bed with an attached metal trapeze system of bars, rings, and hanging apparatus designed to help support daddy with getting in and out of bed.

As usual, mommy was lying on the floor on her left side, propped up on her elbow, watching TV, and smoking. She wore her black polyester pantsuit with its matching vest and a white cotton blouse with a ruffle that peeked out from the vest. To my knowledge, she never went anywhere during the day, so I was always surprised that she was so dressed up when I came home from school.

As I opened our apartment door with my key and walked in, she turned her head away from her daily soap opera and casually asked, "Hi, Pam. How was school?"

"Okay," I replied nonchalantly as I set my notebook, along with my schoolbooks, on the dining room table, carefully placing the keys that I carried on a leather lanyard on top of them.

Purposefully, I ignored the bed and walked into the small kitchen, opened the fridge, and took out a diet Shasta cream soda. This was daddy's favorite flavor and mine, too. We bought cases of it at the local grocery store. As I popped the top of the soda can, pulling the metal piece back to open it, I took a swig of the bubbly, artificially-flavored and -sweetened water. It tasted familiar and refreshing after my walk home.

Leaving the kitchen, it was a little tricky to navigate around the bed that was in the middle of the room. I managed to walk sideways past it, and sat down in a chair next to the couch, across from mommy. She slowly sat up and crossed her legs, placing her lit cigarette in the black plastic ashtray next to where her opened package of cigarettes and plastic lighter lay on the carpet.

"Your dad's new bed came today," she informed me.

No shit! I thought. Is it going to stay in the living room?

"He needs to try it out to make sure he can pull himself up using the equipment."

What if he can't? I wanted to ask.

She continued, "He'll be home soon. You can help him."

Of course, I thought. I can help a two-hundred-fifty-pound wheelchair-bound man climb onto a metal hospital bed. No problem.

Wondering if mommy really believed that I could help him, I looked at the bed more closely. It was raised off the ground about two or three feet. Daddy would need a stool or a few metal stairs to even get onto it. But he couldn't move his legs. How was this going to happen? I decided to ask.

"So how will daddy get in the bed?"

She looked at me and confidently answered, "He'll transfer himself from his chair to the bed. He can use the trapeze to pull himself up."

Will he? I thought. How? The bed is too high and he is too weak. How could she not know this?

When daddy got home from work, I met him in the garage and helped him transfer into his wheelchair. We rode the elevator up together. The smell of urine was stronger than normal as it emanated from the jar which sat poised on his lap.

I'm not sure why, but I decided to tell him about the bed. "Your new bed came today."

"Good," he replied, "I've been waiting for it. Did your mom see it?"

I wanted to scream. How could she miss it?

But I coolly responded, "Yes," then looked straight ahead at the gold-colored elevator buttons.

When the elevator doors opened, daddy whirred down the hallway toward our apartment. I followed his wheelchair, opened the apartment door, and stood behind him as he maneuvered through the doorframe and into the apartment.

Mommy was now standing in the kitchen preparing dinner. It smelled like hamburgers, one of daddy's favorites. Although most nights he ate saltine crackers soaked in milk. Either his appetite, or his ability to digest certain foods, or possibly both, had limited his palate.

Once inside, I took the jar of urine from his lap and walked to the bathroom, where I opened the toilet lids and poured the pungent liquid in, turning my head in disgust. Flushing twice to make sure it was all gone, I washed and dried my hands and returned to the living room.

While I was in the bathroom, daddy had moved his wheelchair next to the bed. His shoulders sat level with the mattress. He looked up at the trapeze of hanging rings and equipment that were fashioned to help hoist him in and out of the bed. What was he thinking? I didn't know, but in that moment, I felt a deep sadness for him. How must it feel to not be able to walk or even move your legs to get in and out of bed? I suddenly realized that he was truly disabled.

The bed was eventually moved into my parents' bedroom by some strong men from the rehabilitation facility. They also lowered the bed enough so daddy, with the help of mommy, was able to hoist himself into the bed using the trapeze to pull himself up.

This lasted for about a month before his condition deteriorated even more and he was placed in a convalescent home, which seemed like such a relief to mommy. As if a huge burden had been taken from her.

I remember her telling me, quite emphatically, "I never have to let him touch me again."

Her words seemed harsh, considering daddy really couldn't move his arms very well. I wondered why it was so important to her to not let him touch her.

• • •

When daddy was moved to the convalescent home, it was close to the apartment where we lived at the time, and he could visit us. Although he was no longer able to drive his Dodge Charger, he was outfitted with a state-of-the-art van, complete with a hydraulic lift for his wheelchair and hand controls. He would pick my little brother up and take him to McDonald's to get burgers, fries, and Cokes. They would sit in the van talking and eating. Then daddy would drop him back off at the apartment. This arrangement lasted for several months, until daddy's condition worsened and he could no longer drive.

So in order to see him, my little brother and I started visiting daddy at the convalescent home. It was probably about a mile walk from our apartment, maybe a little longer, but we'd become accustomed to walking in Los Angeles.

One Saturday afternoon, we left our apartment and headed down the street. When we finally arrived there, we walked up to the entrance, opened the frosted glass doors to the building, and went inside. I wasn't sure where to find daddy since he'd moved rooms since the last time we visited. Luckily, the nurse on duty at the reception desk directed us to his new room, once I gave her his name.

The convalescent home smelled like a mixture of urine and Lysol, and the grayish-white linoleum-tiled floors were stained, making them look dirty. We walked down a short hallway to daddy's room, passing open rooms where very old men and women lay in their beds, or sat in chairs, motionless, watching TV.

As we approached his room, I felt scared. What would he look like? It had only been a couple of weeks since we'd last seen him. I wondered if he'd changed or if he would look worse. Turning the corner, I saw him. He was lying in bed, slightly propped up and covered by a white sheet. He looked the same. I felt relieved. As soon as he saw my little brother and me, a huge smile lit up his face.

"Hi, kids!" he beamed, looking elated to see us.

Then he reached out to both my little brother and me. Not sure how to respond, I walked over toward the bed and leaned down to give him a hug. My little brother followed suit. His bed had a similar trapeze setup to the one that had been delivered to our apartment. He reached up and held onto one of the rings, and pulled himself up to a seated position.

My little brother and I didn't really know what to say, so daddy did most of the talking. He told us about the food they served him, and the songs he liked to listen to on the small beige-colored clock radio that mommy had bought for him. He loved Barry Manilow's popular music, especially the song, "I Write the Songs." He thought it sounded like a Scientologist wrote it, because of the lyrics:

"I've been alive forever. And I wrote the very first song."

While we were there, one of the orderlies, a large, muscular black man in blue scrubs, came into the room. "How we doin' today, Mr. Nickel?" he asked jovially.

Daddy smiled broadly as he replied, "Great! My kids came to visit."

He introduced us and told the man our ages. My little brother and I were both painfully shy. We looked down at the linoleum floor and mumbled hello.

The man smiled and told daddy, "I'll be back around in a bit for your exercises. Ya'll keep visitin'."

After the orderly left the room, I turned to daddy and told him that we needed to leave, but promised that we'd be back next week. I'm not sure if I knew that was true, but I didn't want him to feel sad when we left.

I watched as his face changed. His smile faded and he lowered himself back into the bed. My little brother and I gave him one more hug before we left. Then we both waved to him as we walked out of the room.

He waved back and said, "Thanks for coming, kids. I'll see you next week."

Walking with my little brother out of the convalescent doors, I wanted to cry. Daddy was alone. He'd never come home again. But I knew, in mommy's defense, she couldn't provide the full-time care that he needed: toileting, bathing, and moving him from his wheelchair to his bed and back again. Walking back to our apartment, I tried not to think about it.

⸺⟋⟍⸺

DADDY'S
SCIENTOLOGY WINS

Although daddy didn't go with us to Saint Hill in England, he did receive auditing and training when we first arrived in Los Angeles. He must have taken courses at night and on the weekends, because he worked during the day.

Once he was wheelchair-bound, he briefly continued to take courses at Celebrity Centre, using hand controls to drive his Dodge Charger to and from the Org. He loved mingling with fellow Scientologists, who seemed astounded by his ability to be cheerful and positive despite his illness.

His Social Security Disability checks may have helped fund his training and auditing, but he was only able to complete the lower OT levels before becoming totally incapacitated. Daddy even purchased personalized license plates that read "GO OT," which referred to

"Operating Thetan," his attained level of Scientology enlightenment up the "Bridge to Total Freedom."

His OT "wins," as they were called, were even published in one of Scientology's magazines, *Advance!* The publication was mailed and distributed to Scientologists who were not only interested in moving up L. Ron Hubbard's "Bridge to Total Freedom," but who were also willing to spend enormous amounts of money to learn the OT secrets of the Church.

Higher OT levels promised Scientology members the ability to leave their bodies and perform all sorts of amazing feats using the powers they achieved as they moved from one OT level to the next. Daddy's testimonial convinced me that he wholeheartedly believed he possessed special powers:

Advance! Issue 20—August/September 1973

One day while watching a live soccer game on television I became aware of the clouds overhead my house and began pushing them around. This was fun. Then I became aware of the clouds at the location of the soccer game and began moving them around, mostly to make the sun shine on the soccer game. Then I found a new game. I flowed a theta flow to the players on each team and the results were fantastic. The tempo of the game doubled and the players kicked the ball twice as far as they had been kicking it. Then I stopped the flow. The game went back to normal. Then I started the flow and the tempo of the game again doubled.

Paul Nickel—OT

After reading daddy's account of his newfound OT abilities, I was a bit bewildered. Mostly because I couldn't ever remember daddy watching a soccer game, or any sporting event for that matter. Maybe an occasional football game, but he really wasn't a big sports fan.

Secondly, and probably more importantly, I thought, if daddy possessed these amazing powers that allowed him to control the clouds, as well as the outcomes of a soccer game, why couldn't he cure his MS, or at the very least "flow a theta flow," whatever that meant, to his legs and get them working again?

Herein lies the predicament. Scientologists don't have superpowers, nor can they control the universe. Despite all of L. Ron Hubbard's promises, lies, and absurd proposed truths, Scientology doesn't create superior beings who can "Clear the planet."

Instead, Scientology preys on gullible individuals, like my parents, who were swept up in the allure of changing the world and in the notion that as Scientologists, they would become not only happier, but also more able and capable.

Yet even when daddy's legs and hands were useless, atrophied by the debilitating effects of MS, he still proudly wore his Scientology Clear Bracelet. It was tangible proof of his accomplishment and evidence that he was a true believer and follower, in spite of his deteriorated physical state.

Once, when I asked daddy about his bracelet, he explained to me how he purchased it after becoming "Clear." He specifically showed me where the inscription stated his Clear number. On the other side of the bracelet was the Scientology symbol of the letter "S" with slightly raised overlayed triangles. He explained that the triangles represented Affinity, Reality, and Communication.

Like a Medal of Honor, his bracelet symbolized daddy's Scientology journey and his perceived attainment of freedom. Perhaps spiritually, he felt free. Yet physically, daddy would never walk or be able to move his body by himself ever again.

LEARNING ABOUT DADDY

Not long after mommy placed daddy in the convalescent facility, she decided to share something disturbing. It was about daddy. I guess, in her mind, she thought I was old enough to hear the information, or maybe she just needed someone to talk to because daddy was gone. Whatever the reason, mommy proceeded to tell me about some Scientology friends they'd visited before moving to Colorado.

According to mommy, these friends, Wayne and Wendy, were free spirits who lived in San Diego and worked at the local Scientology franchise. They'd both been in D.C., with my parents, pretty much from the beginning of Scientology's founding. Mommy was convinced that daddy's interest in Wayne began in the shadows at the Hubbard Association of Scientologists' conventions they all attended.

She told me it happened years before when she and Wendy were outside their D.C., apartment, with me and another Scientologist who also had a one-year-old toddler. Daddy and Wayne were upstairs in the apartment. Mommy believed, because there was no one to stop them, or judge them, except their wives, who weren't present, that daddy and Wayne had the opportunity, the freedom to entertain a liaison. When she confronted daddy about what she thought had happened, he admitted it to her. He and Wayne had sex.

At the end of her tale, she took a long drag on her cigarette and looked out the sliding glass window at the balcony outside our apartment. I sat silently on the carpet in front of the TV trying to comprehend what she'd just told me. Heterosexual relationships between a man and a woman, like my parents, was my only sexual frame of reference. I didn't have any context for understanding what mommy was telling me.

Soon after we arrived in California, even before daddy got sick, his bedroom "visits" had stopped, more than likely because his sexual urges were starting to diminish due to the beginning stages of his illness. I'd also buried my memories of the secrets that daddy and I shared back in Denver and Slidell.

As defined by L. Ron Hubbard in his book, *Dianetics: The Modern Science of Mental Health*:

> "*The sexual pervert (and by this term Dianetics, to be brief, includes any and all forms of deviation in Dynamic II such as homosexuality, lesbianism, sexual sadism, etc.)...is actually quite ill physically. Perversion as an illness has so many manifestations that it must be spread through the entire gamut of classes.... And*

the sum of it is that the pervert is always a very ill person in one way or another, whether he is conscious of it or not. He is very far from culpable for his condition, but he is also so far from normal and so extremely dangerous to society that the tolerance of perversion is as thoroughly bad for society as punishment for it."

Scientology doctrine clearly addresses sexual behavior. Homosexuality and bisexuality had no place in Scientology. Mommy knew this.

After sharing her story, Mommy and I sat in silence for a few minutes. Then she turned to me and said, quite matter-of-factly, "Pam, your father is bisexual."

I looked at her quizzically and replied, "What does that mean?"

A small smile appeared on her face as she puffed on her cigarette. Not enough to show her dimple, but enough to let me know she was amused by my question.

"Well, Pam," she said rather smugly, "It's when men have sex with each other."

Although I wasn't yet sexually active, I did know a thing or two about how sex happened from watching TV and from talking to my friends. My mind began to picture men having sex, and not just men, but daddy. This was too much!

I stood up and tried to pretend that I hadn't heard her explanation. Walking toward the bathroom, I told her I was going to take a shower.

As I took a few steps, she continued in a defensive tone of voice, "Pam, I only told you because you're old enough now to know about your father."

And then she made her final statement, "How do you think I felt? It wasn't easy for me. I had to live with him."

I stopped walking and turned around to look at her. She sat cross-legged on the carpet. I'm not sure why, but mommy rarely sat in chairs. Holding her cigarette to her lips, she inhaled deeply, then let out the smoke in my direction.

I wanted to yell at her and tell her it wasn't true. Daddy couldn't do what she was describing. Then it occurred to me that she was telling me this because daddy was gone, and she didn't have anyone to love her anymore. She wanted me to feel sorry for her. But I didn't. I couldn't. If I felt sorry for anyone, it was daddy, not mommy. He was the one who was sick, frail, and powerless.

⸺◦⊱⊰◦⸺

MOMMY FINDS A JOB

With daddy no longer able to work and provide for us, mommy had to rally, and quickly, if she wanted us to survive and not succumb to a life of poverty.

So, miraculously, without the help of Scientology or any Scientologists, she gradually, of her own volition, overcame her agoraphobia and found a job about a mile away from our apartment in the Mid-Wilshire, Los Angeles.

The process of leaving the apartment and getting back out into the world was both gradual and painstaking for her. Recreating herself as a competent and organized woman who possessed clerical skills, such as taking dictation, typing, and filing, required referencing past work experience.

For a brief period of time after we moved to the new apartment, mommy transcribed documents for ASHO, just a few blocks away. She would listen to tapes, of what I'm not sure, and then type up the notes on the IBM Selectric typewriter she'd purchased.

I'm honestly not sure how she was able to convince a legal firm that she possessed previous paralegal experience, but she did. Maybe she listed the Church of Scientology as her previous employer.

Sitting at the kitchen table, poised in front of her typewriter, I watched her carefully complete a job application in between smoked cigarettes. Then she rolled the paper out by turning the knob on the side, checking it methodically for any typos. Mommy could be meticulous when it came to typing and putting words on paper.

With a full ashtray of cigarette butts and ashes next to the typewriter, she folded up the application, carefully placed it in a legal-sized envelope, which she licked shut and then addressed. After placing a six-cent postage stamp in the right top corner, I watched her leave the apartment, envelope in hand.

She must have walked down the long hallway to the elevator, then taken it downstairs to the first floor where the gold-colored mailboxes lined the wall. "Outgoing Mail" was written above the narrow slot where mail was inserted.

I'm not sure how many job applications mommy sent out, but eventually she received a phone call from a legal firm in an office building less than a mile from our apartment. Excited and nervous, mommy shared the news with me one day after I'd come home from school. She told me the office was in the Bullocks Wilshire building, an iconic Los Angeles landmark that housed offices as well as the expensive Bullock's department store.

Mommy had started shopping there, mostly ordering dresses and outfits for me by phone, after seeing their fashion advertisements in the *L.A. Times* newspaper. Due to her agoraphobia, she didn't venture out to stores much.

I wasn't sure how she afforded to buy clothing from such an expensive store, but the prices didn't seem to deter her. Maybe the Disability checks that daddy received were enough to cover rent, food, and these extravagances.

Or, more likely, since my parents were no longer spending large sums of money on Scientology services, they had a bit more discretionary income to spend. Mommy probably rationalized her clothing expenses as necessary. Her job interview definitely required the purchase of a new dress!

Once she learned she'd been hired, her next purchase was a car. Although the office was less than a mile from our apartment, she couldn't walk there comfortably in a dress and heels. So, one day, a light-yellow VW Bug appeared in the parking garage. Mommy proudly showed off her "new" car to me and my little brother, telling us she'd purchased it from a Scientologist who worked at ASHO.

Even though she was no longer active in Scientology, she'd kept in touch with a few Scientologists at the Org. Perhaps one of them needed money and an exchange was made, no questions asked. Or maybe this was her way of staying connected to Scientology but on her own terms.

I felt shocked and somewhat fearful that mommy would now be driving to work every day. What if she panicked or couldn't remember how to drive? I thought. Her new behavior seemed foreign to me. But it was apparent that she was taking more control over her life, even accepting the hand she'd been dealt, as best she could.

MY SCIENTOLOGY PATH,
CIRCA 1971-1972

T hirteen was the magical age for everything. At least that is what I believed and began planning for. Freedom to ride the bus alone in the city, and freedom to have sex. These were the two most important events that I was certain would change my life.

Before turning thirteen, I'd never really engaged in Scientology training or auditing myself, aside from a children's Communication Course that I participated in at Saint Hill, which I didn't remember. But mommy had saved the paper certificate I received as proof.

My indoctrination began the summer before I started junior high school. I was volunteered by my parents to help at the newly-opened Scientology Org, Celebrity Centre, where Yvonne Gillham Jentzsch, who was Scientology royalty, had been handpicked by L. Ron Hubbard to oversee its success.

I'm not sure if both mommy and daddy made the arrangements or if just mommy made the call to Yvonne, but daddy definitely supported the idea, voicing his opinion from his bed at the convalescent home.

In actuality though, I may have been chosen because neither one of my parents were actively taking courses or receiving auditing at that time, or in other words, paying good money to the Church, so I became the target. But I was excited! Walking by myself to Celebrity Centre was literally, in my mind, the first step in gaining my freedom.

Although I volunteered at Celebrity Centre, I also frequently visited or stopped in at AOLA, the Advanced Organization in Los Angeles, which was housed in an old Craftsman-style home in the Westlake neighborhood near downtown Los Angeles.

The Orgs, as they were called, were usually housed in cheap properties that were in older, poor neighborhoods. To get there, I walked through MacArthur Park and then up a few blocks to Alvarado Boulevard. It took me about thirty or forty minutes if I didn't stop at the local liquor store for candy and a soda.

As I walked down Alvarado Boulevard, I peered at the window displays in all the little shops. In 1972, these shops were a mixture of Mexican tiendas alongside stores that had been in business since the 1950s. They were mom-and-pop shops. While window-shopping, I'd dream of what I could buy when I was older and in the Sea Org making money.

My daydreams included leaving mommy, my little brother, and daddy, even though he was sick, to live a much more glamourous life. Little did I know the meager amount of money that Sea Org Scientologists were paid, less than minimum wage.

Yet at thirteen years old, just barely past puberty, I desperately wanted to look like so many of the young auditors I saw at Celebrity Centre and AOLA. One particular girl, named Keith, was my idol. First of all, I loved that she was a girl with a boy's name. In my young mind, she was just so cool!

She always wore tight hip-hugger jeans shimmied over a short-sleeved brown leotard. On her feet, she wore wooden and leather clogs, and her wrists and neckline were adorned with beads. Her naturally-curly brown hair fell to her shoulders and framed her exotic face. When she smiled, her eyes crinkled around the edges and you could see a visible gap between her two front teeth.

Her smile seemed both genuine and warm, not like she was hiding anything like so many Scientologists I met at the Orgs. Although probably a bit older than most of the twenty-year-old auditors, she seemed like a true free spirit! I wanted to BE her.

Finally, after walking many long blocks, I reached my destination, Celebrity Centre. Originally located at Eighth Street and Burlington, it was housed in an old wooden building that had been purchased and then repurposed into a Scientology hub for attracting actors, actresses, musicians, and artists.

A huge portrait of L. Ron Hubbard, bigger than life, covered an entire wall at Celebrity Centre. Just his head and shoulders. His hand rested under his chin, a bit like Rodin's sculpture of *The Thinker*. Looking thoughtful, wise, and all-knowing.

His gaze was poised and piercing, and like the *Mona Lisa*, his eyes seemed to follow you wherever you walked in the room. Omniscient and omnipresent, like a God, he watched over his disciples. After all, Scientology was a religion.

Yet even at Celebrity Centre, where actors like John Travolta first became involved, Scientology preyed on the downtrodden and those with "ruins" that could be identified and lured into a cheap training course entitled the Communication Course. Young twenty-year-old Sea Org members signed-up broken and curious people who wandered by the building, like the blind man I was to "communicate" with.

Maybe thirty years old, possibly older, the blind man had stringy long brown hair and a long brown beard, with blue eyes that looked like someone had poured milk into them. Sky-blue orbs that floated in a sea of milky-white liquid. Large and round. Cloudy and unseeing. No dark glasses to hide them. Surrounded by thick lids with dark-brown lashes.

I was assigned to "run" the communication drills with him. Probably because the young Sea Org guys who signed-up "walk-ins" were jerks and didn't care if it was me, a young girl, a kid, who had to look at his cloudy, blue, unseeing eyes for hours on end. They knew I wouldn't complain.

After all, this was Celebrity Centre, where important Scientologists like Travolta (not yet famous) and Kenny Lipton, the brother of Peggy Lipton (*Mod Squad*-famous) came to get trained and audited. What would they think if they were paired up, as required for the communication drills, with a blind man? What might happen if either one of them had to stare at those eyes for hours without blinking?

So it was me and the blind man. We sat on hard gray metal folding chairs, the kind you stick to when the backs of your thighs get too sweaty. Our knees didn't touch, but almost. We both rested our hands on the tops of our thighs, palms down, per the drill protocol.

Seated directly across from the blind man, I started the drill. "Do birds fly?"

He responded, "Yes."

Then I asked him, "Do fish swim?"

Again, he responded, "Yes."

We were robotic. We followed the drill and repeated the commands, as they are referred to, over and over and over and over, for what seemed like an eternity.

"Do birds fly?"

"Do fish swim?"

I didn't question the commands. I didn't even think. What nonsense! I just did what I'd been taught.

One of the purposes of the communication drill was to remain calm, focused, and unflustered as the questions were repeated over and over again. The drill's repetition was to train Scientologists to get their question answered despite any efforts from the other person to distract them.

Ironically, the blind man's opaque blue eyes were unable to see me or the other people in the room, yet he kept his gaze directed at me. He appeared to be fully present. But never having seen a blind man's eyes before, I felt a bit uncomfortable. I wondered why he didn't wear glasses, like I'd seen on TV, to protect his eyes.

Finally, after several rounds of the nonsense commands and responses, we switched roles and he questioned me.

"Do birds fly?"

"Do fish swim?"

Each time I replied, "Yes," with a slightly different intonation.

The drill was tedious, and I didn't want to look at his eyes any longer. I honestly wondered what these drills and questions had to do with communication.

Tired and bored, I quickly glanced over at the young guys who had assigned us to be partners. They were chatting and laughing. I felt like I was part of their fun. Were they laughing at me or at the spectacle of the two of us? A child and a scraggly-bearded blind man who sat transfixed, compliantly asking each other absurd questions. Perhaps their amusement had more to do with control, and more specifically with learning to control others, L. Ron Hubbard's primary goal.

But at thirteen, I was happier there, in the training room with the blind man and the young guys, than I was in our apartment with mommy. Anything really was better than that. I felt grown-up when I was at Celebrity Centre. Mostly because I was treated like an adult, and told that I was smart, wise, and capable.

One day, while at Celebrity Centre, an older male Scientologist confirmed my hopes. During our brief, animated conversation, he told me, "Man, you've lived before this life! You picked your parents so you could get this tech from Ron. Too bad you're in a young body right now. But when you're older, we'll get married. It's cool."

Flattered, I thought, Yeah, it's cool. I can't wait until I'm older. I absolutely believed and hoped for this magical thinking to be true.

MY SCIENTOLOGY
TRAINING & AUDITING

My Scientology grooming continued throughout the summer.
Possibly after proving that I could "handle" the drills without
"caving in," a Scientology term for "falling apart," I was assigned my
next training task.

Walking up the hill on Third Street, and then two blocks over
to Beverly Boulevard, I reached Karla's apartment. She was an older
Scientologist, maybe in her fifties. She was Sandy's mother. Sandy
was a trainer, kind of like a teacher, at Celebrity Centre.

Karla spoke with an accent. I think she was Scandinavian, but
I'm not sure. I'd been assigned to train with her, to be her partner.
Sandy told me to meet her mother at her apartment, because neither
one of us drove, and then walk with her to Celebrity Centre.

Once we arrived, after our twenty-minute walk, we checked
in and found our seats in the course room, where we diligently

read the LRH training bulletins for the Student Study Course. Using our little "tool kits," composed of paper clips, pennies, and other assorted small objects, including slabs of gray clay, we would "demo" or demonstrate our understanding of words and concepts to each other.

Rolling small bits of gray clay into little round balls, I placed them on top of each other to form two snowmen people. It was like playing with Play-Doh. I drew eyes and mouths on each one using a paperclip that I'd unwound, and placed them on the training table facing each other. To convey talking, I rolled more bits of clay into long snakes and fashioned speech bubbles next to each snowman person. Clearly, you could tell they were "talking" to each other. Karla immediately identified that I understood the term communication.

Karla placed pennies and paperclips together, and then pulled them apart to create the definition of the term "disconnect." Thetan was always a good one. Karla would roll the gray clay into little balls and ropes, carefully molding them together to create a tiny person. Then she would add a small round rope circle around the clay person's head. It reminded me of an angel. I learned quickly that this was her concept of "a being" or "thetan," Scientology's version of a "soul."

Just thirteen years old, I coached and trained with Karla, a woman old enough to be my mother and possibly my grandmother. Once, when Karla shared her understanding of a particular passage we were reading, I corrected her pronunciation of one of the Scientology terms. Her accent was sometimes thick, and I wanted her to learn the right way to say it.

She looked at me, eyebrows raised, but she didn't balk. She just repeated the term, as best she could, trying hard to say it correctly. Afterward, I thought, honestly, it sounds better when she says it her way. But I was a compliant trainee and I knew we were being watched.

Karla and I were an odd pairing, but in that Scientology course room, size and age were irrelevant. A thetan was a thetan, no matter how young or old. Besides, I liked Karla. She always packed a lunch that she shared with me. Such a sweet woman. She was the kind of mother, or grandmother, I wished for. Nice, but not overly sweet or emotional.

She also treated me as somewhat of an equal, although I'm sure it must have been difficult for her, when the arrangement was first proposed, to agree to train with a young teenager. Perhaps her daughter, Sandy, had persuaded her, or Yvonne, the head of Celebrity Centre.

Each day, Sandy stopped by and checked on us to make sure we were reading and progressing at a sufficient pace through the course material: bulletins and policies typed in green, blue, or red ink, depending on their importance.

Scientology was not only about signing people up for training and auditing, but also about moving them through quickly, so they could buy the next book, level of training, or package of auditing sessions, even if the people were your family.

After training, as devoted Scientologists, we sat in chairs at Celebrity Centre, listening to Yvonne, our leader, share important information with us. Stats, successes, and motivational words.

Yvonne also spoke of Celebrity Centre's purpose, telling us

that CC, as it was also called, was dedicated to all the artists who came through its doors. Celebrity Centre's mission was to take care of them so they would have a place where they could express themselves freely and grow, sharing their contributions with society and the world.

Celebrity Centre was definitely a "special project" to bring celebrities, along with their money, into Scientology. I fondly remember Yvonne greeting me each day at Celebrity Centre with her lovely Australian accent in her sunny, friendly manner. She was always so positive!

By choice that day, I sat next to Ray, who was seated next to Gelda, his girlfriend. She was blonde, maybe not naturally, and bigger-boned than Ray. She looked Swedish or German to my untrained, teenage eyes. I thought her face looked a bit like a model's, with a squarish jaw and white porcelain skin. She wore long flowing skirts and dresses that made her resemble a '70s flower child.

Ray was nineteen years old sporting a peach fuzz moustache. He looked like a cowboy, boots and all. Tall and lanky with wavy, longish brown 1970s hair that lay loosely at his shoulders on top of his Western shirt with snaps instead of buttons. He sat picking his teeth with a toothpick, chewing on it really. Self-assured, yet naïve. A young kid from money. One of three sons from a prominent Texan family who chose a rebellious path.

Sitting next to Ray, I felt shy, but also bold. "Hi Ray," I said casually.

He looked at me and answered, "Hi."

After listening to Yvonne's updates, some people, including

Gelda, got up and walked back to their jobs, or "posts," as they were referred to. But Ray sat there a little longer.

This was my opportunity to talk to Ray, one on one. Mustering my courage, I decided to speak. "So, how's Gelda?"

Ray was coy and quiet when I asked him about Gelda, as if I, a young teenager, had the right to know about his girlfriend. Smirking under his light-brown peach fuzz, the corners of his pinkish lips curled up ever so slightly. I was amusing him.

But it seemed like he was feeling playful, so I continued questioning him. "She's your girlfriend, isn't she?"

As I waited for his response, I saw Gelda walking back toward us. She was close enough to hear my question. She listened but kept her poker face. Maybe no one was supposed to know they were together, but I definitely wanted to know. Mostly because I had a crush on Ray.

He was tall, cute, and closer to my age than many of the Scientologists at Celebrity Centre. He also was newly-arrived, and interesting, in a reserved and secretive way. He spoke very little, and seemed to sit back and take it all in. More an observer than an outspoken member. He sparked my curiosity.

I even imagined him as my boyfriend. My magical thinking allowed me to truly believe I was as desirable as his beautiful twenty-something-year-old girlfriend. Clearly, I was a child and she was a woman. But as a Scientologist, I wholeheartedly believed what I'd been told, that I was a thetan, equal to any other thetan, but just in a young body. But in reality, I was jailbait, and certainly not what Ray had come to California to find, although Ray did take care of me once.

. . .

Only thirteen years old, I'd never tasted, nor drunk champagne before, especially cheap André Champagne, and in the middle of the afternoon.

Ray and I had both been at the "party" to celebrate Celebrity Centre's auditing success numbers. I enjoyed being part of these celebrations. The staff at the Orgs were always so excited when the stats were read aloud. They truly believed they were making a difference in the world.

Maybe because he knew I'd drunk too much champagne, or maybe because I asked him to, Ray drove me home to my apartment. After watching me stumble up the stairs, he witnessed me throw up all over the glass front door that led into the foyer of the apartment complex. With little hesitation, he turned, walked back to his car, and drove away, leaving me at the top of the stairs. Job done. He'd successfully delivered me to my destination. But even though I was sick, I felt special, even desirable, because Ray had driven me home.

Eventually, while at Celebrity Centre, Ray became one of my auditors, which I enjoyed, because I got to spend time with him, even though it was limited. Listening to him ask me auditing questions and responding with what I presumed were the "right" answers also made me feel grown-up.

As an auditor, Ray was a good listener, empathetic, and unflappable. Not surprising, he went on to become one of the top echelon Sea Org leaders, even auditing L. Ron Hubbard during his final years.

. . .

But paradoxically, the more I became involved in Scientology, the more I learned about its inner workings and insidious tactics.

Although Scientology advertised itself as a religion, I began to see that it was really a business. A factory of freedom. Case folders filled with notes of ailments, problems, actions, and reactions, written by auditors and their supervisors. The case supervisor was the demigod who deemed the next steps. More auditing, different questions. Ongoing and expensive. Scientology was always about production and increasing numbers, which equated to sales.

And as its leader, L. Ron Hubbard was always writing and creating new "technology." The word "technology" was used freely in the 1970s. But the concept of technology, in Scientology jargon, was futuristic. It didn't connect to any true technology, except for possibly the e-meter, which Scientologists still use today.

About the size of a small laptop computer, the e-meter is basically a box that houses a small screen covered with glass, which displays a black needle that can move loosely between measured increments, somewhat like a car speedometer.

As a Scientologist, I learned that the e-meter's purpose is to register a member's reactions to questions and revelations during auditing. The pre-Clear, a Scientologist who has not yet attained a state of Clear, which means your reactive mind is still controlling your thoughts and actions, holds tin cans, the kind that resemble soup cans, in the palm of each hand. The cans are connected to the e-meter through a plastic-coated wire with an electrode (metal piece) that plugs into a jack on the side of the e-meter.

Through my training courses, I also began to understand that Scientology's espoused "tech," written solely by LRH, was printed in various colors to denote its importance, distribution, and enforcement. Hubbard's bulletins, policies, and commanding orders, which were typed and distributed only according to his specific and precise directions, created the framework for consistency, as well as his dogmatic and autocratic control of the organization, and thus its followers. No one questioned LRH. His words were considered true and absolute.

During the early 1970s, the delivery of Hubbard's new "tech" was practiced by Sea Org auditors who were trained on Scientology's ship, the *Apollo*, formerly the *Royal Scotman*, and at local Orgs called Flag Land Bases. These highly trained Sea Org members were revered.

The delivery and purpose of this new "tech" was publicized under the guise of Scientology's altruistic purpose of Clearing the planet and creating superior beings. Yet in Scientology Orgs worldwide, these "superior beings," like my parents, became consumers who continued to pay large sums of money to become "freer" and more enlightened.

Each week, the number of courses completed, along with levels of attainment, were shared and celebrated in each Org. However, the results were just a devised hierarchy of levels that L. Ron Hubbard created to incentivize payments in order to financially milk his besotted followers.

Once the cult mentality took hold, and hundreds and thousands of dollars had been expended, there was no turning back. This is what happened to my parents. They were in too deep.

I realized this one day while looking through a Scientology magazine that lay on the kitchen counter in our apartment. As I flipped through the magazine, I saw this advertisement for Advanced Course Donations:

ADVANCED COURSE DONATIONS
Clearing Course – $800.00
($760.00 – 5% advance payment discount price)

TOTAL POWER PACKAGE (OT I – OT VIII)***
$3,000.00 ($2,850.00)

*Plus $200.00 for special auditing by a Class VIII auditor – no discount

**Plus any extra fee for special auditing actions.
A minimum of 5 hours for $150.00 (no discount)
is purchased at the start of the level.

***Package prices do not include special auditing on OT IV and OT VII.

ADVANCED COURSES ONCE ATTESTED ARE 50% OF ORIGINAL FEE IF RETREADED.

Make your check or money order payable to "AOLA."

I was shocked! I had no idea my parents had been paying this much money for Scientology courses and auditing. I wondered, Did they have to pay additional fees for mommy to have special auditing, on top of the $3,000 price tag for daddy's OT levels? I also wondered why the services were considered "donations" to be paid by check or money order when the prices were clearly marked.

As a teenager, without a job, hundreds and thousands of dollars seemed like a fortune. And in the 1970s, these "donations" were substantial, even exorbitant for some individuals and families, like my own.

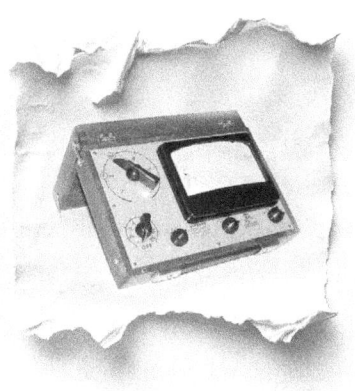

SCIENTOLOGY ORG LIFE,
CIRCA 1972–1973

Although LRH and Mary Sue Hubbard, his wife, did not condone premarital sex, it was happening a lot. I learned firsthand, while receiving Scientology auditing, that the concept of free love from the 1960s was still being practiced in Scientology.

Housing arrangements for those who lived at the Orgs was not coed. But shacking up, or living together, in the small number of rooms that existed in the old Craftsman homes that housed Sea Org Scientologists in Los Angeles, facilitated some sharing. This occurred in the form of dormitories that were same-sex, and often in the form of couples, some married, but many not.

Steve, an older Scientology auditor, possible in his thirties, had established a lucrative living arrangement, which included a live-in Scientology girlfriend. Steve was smooth. A good talker and a good listener. He could probably sell you just about anything, a perfect fit for Scientology. He was also nice-looking, in a dark-haired, smooth-talking, "let me help you" kind of way.

Steve wasn't married, and he definitely enjoyed the selection of young girls who had joined the Scientology Org in Los Angeles. He'd conveniently worked out a very amicable living arrangement with a beautiful young Scientologist who was probably barely eighteen years old. I believe she had a younger sister as well, whom unfortunately for him, he couldn't touch yet.

One afternoon, after an auditing session, I visited Steve's room. I was just thirteen. One of the protocols, after receiving auditing, was to have another auditor attest to your "floating needle." A "floating needle" could be observed using the e-meter, a device that allegedly shows evidence of emotional states of being.

Basically, a "floating needle" was a quality control feature of Scientology that documented the auditor's success in bringing the pre-Clear, someone who hadn't yet attained a state of enlightenment, to a serene and happy emotional state at the end of the auditing session. Attesting to this evidence was one of Steve's jobs, although he was also an auditor.

Sitting in his auditing room, which also doubled as his living quarters, I sat at a wooden table across from Steve, holding the tin cans that were connected to his e-meter. I had been sent to him to verify my successful auditing session. As I walked into the room to sit down at the table, I noted that the waterbed that he shared with his girlfriend was wobbling ever so slightly, as evidenced by the subtle movement of the dark-colored blanket that sat on top of the water mattress.

His girlfriend walked out of the bathroom and looked at Steve.

He smiled and nodded at her. I stared at her. I was not only taken aback by her beauty, but also by the fact that she was in the room. I was pretty sure I'd interrupted their afternoon fun.

Looking directly at me, he coyly stated, "This is Julie."

Dressed in a very short miniskirt, which barely covered her behind, she waved at me and said, "Hi," as she walked over to him, kissed him squarely on the lips, and strode confidently out the door, closing it behind her.

Steve smiled at me and leaned in toward his e-meter as he shared, "It's great to be able to grab a quickie in the afternoon, between sessions."

Shocked by their open display of affection in an auditing room, and unsure of the term "quickie," but grasping its implications, I blushed. A deep-pink crept into my cheeks. Without skipping a beat, Steve looked at me intently over the top of his e-meter and asked me a few questions, following the prescribed protocol, as directed by LRH policy.

I wondered if my needle would float? Hopefully, or I'd be sent back to the auditing session, or scheduled for more auditing, until it occurred. I always tried to think of something happy or something good, something that I liked, during this process. I stared at Steve, answered the questions, and thought, I wonder what it would be like to kiss him? Steve thanked me for my answers, as he was taught to do, and glanced down at the e-meter.

Beaming at me, he stated, "Thank you. Your needle is floating."

Thank goodness! We were done. Although what I really wanted was to stay in this man's room, without his girlfriend, and talk to him some more.

He jotted down a few quick notes on the white piece of unlined paper that was poised inside my manila pre-Clear folder. He was left-handed, and I watched him pick up his blue pen, and scrawl sideways on the paper. I found it interesting as I'd really never seen someone write left-handed before.

Quickly, he finished writing, clicked the pen to hide the ink tip, closed the folder, and tucked it under his arm as he stood up. Putting the cans down on the table, I smiled at him and we walked silently to the door. He opened it and gestured for me to walk out first as he followed, shutting the door behind him. We walked a few feet together to the end of the hallway where there was a window seat.

Steve wasn't a tall man, probably about five-feet-eight, give or take an inch. He seemed shorter than mommy, who lamented to me on many occasions, "All the tall boys always dated these tiny little short girls, leaving me with few choices in college." As if that explained why she'd married daddy, who was five-feet-ten-inches tall.

Mustering all my courage, I looked up at Steve and whispered, "Can I talk to you?"

He looked down at me curiously, "Sure. Let's sit down."

As he sat down on the window seat, covered with a thin blue cushion, he motioned for me to sit next to him. Shyly, I positioned myself across from him on the small seat that was really more like an inside ledge next to a picture window in the old Craftsman home.

He crossed one leg over the other, forming a rectangle. His blue pants rose up ever so slightly above his dark-blue socks, revealing a white ankle covered in dark-black hair. Carefully he twisted the end of his small black moustache that covered his upper lip. When he opened his pink lips to speak, they revealed his fairly straight, but somewhat yellow-stained teeth. Most Scientologists at the Orgs smoked pretty heavily, and he was no exception.

"So what did you want to talk about?" he asked nonchalantly.

Excited that we were sitting so close to each other, but nervous that Scientologists who were walking by might hear our conversation, I whispered, "I want to know how to not be a virgin."

His eyes smiled, but his lips stayed neutral. He had developed a good poker face from his years of training as an auditor.

Speaking slowly, he stated, "Well, first you have to have sex with someone." Then he asked, "Have you ever had sex with anyone?"

Feeling the heat rise from my neck to the top of my head, I blushed, probably turning several shades of pink.

But not wanting to stop this important conversation, with a handsome male Scientologist, I answered, "No, I haven't had sex with anyone."

Technically, this was a true statement.

Amused but maintaining his poker face, Steve responded by asking, "Okay. Well, do you know anyone that you want to have sex with?"

I couldn't believe it! Had he read my mind? Did he know I wanted to have sex with him? Images of him kissing me and laying me down on his waterbed whirred around in my head. Should I tell him?

As I sat silently across from him, looking down at my hands resting on the knees of my blue jeans, I felt exhilarated yet unsure.

We sat in silence for a few seconds. Then he looked at me quizzically, probably trying to read my body language.

Finally, he interrupted the silence and asked, "Do you know any boys your age who would have sex with you?"

Crestfallen, I stammered, somewhat embarrassed, "No, I don't have a boyfriend."

Bravely, I continued. What did I have to lose? This was my opportunity to say what I wanted. Wasn't Scientology all about postulating and taking action to attain "Total Freedom?" I was certain that not being a virgin at thirteen would not only bring me freedom, but also allow me to be viewed as more of an equal in Scientology instead of just a thetan in a young body.

In my small, childlike voice, I looked at him and said, "Steve, I want to have sex with you. I want you to make me not a virgin anymore."

Calmly, he uncrossed his leg and shifted his body weight, almost as if he was getting ready to stand up. Reaching for my hand, which was poised on my right knee, he placed the palm of his warm hand on top of mine. His fingers were long. Small tufts of black hair covered the skin below his knuckles and on the top of his hand.

Not skipping a beat, he was cool, but not condescending. Flattered, I'm sure, he replied, "Pam, I get it. You don't want to be a virgin."

In a serious tone, he continued, "I'd love to have sex with you, but I can't be the first."

Seeing the disappointment written all over my face, he said, "Hey, I'm sure you can find a boyfriend who will have sex with you.

Then you can come back and we can talk some more."

Give her hope, but don't risk the good thing that you have going right now. Jailbait is not worth it, were undoubtedly some of his thoughts. Lifting his hand from mine, he smoothed his dark-black hair back with it as he stood up.

Grinning, he added, "I want to hear all about it when it happens."

Sure, I thought. Both hopeful and determined, I stood up and walked out of the Org and headed back to my apartment building. Finding a boyfriend would be my next step. But first, I became a Scientology auditor.

• • •

I don't have specific memories of my training to become an auditor, or how it was decided that I should become one. But as an auditor, I felt like a true Scientologist, and the fate of others' success on the "Road to Total Freedom" became part of my identity.

However, even though I was fourteen years old, I was still very shy, introverted, and soft-spoken. Yet my confidence emerged as I sat across the table from adults who held tin cans and told me their secrets. I felt important, adult-like, and part of a club.

During one very memorable auditing session, a young woman, of her own volition, took off her sweater, revealing two large, ample breasts. She stated, somewhat adamantly, that she was feeling warm, and that possibly the needle of the e-meter might be affected. She pulled her knitted top over her head, smoothed out her long, dark hair, picked the cans back up, and looked at me intently, as she asked quite seriously, "Is that helping?"

My fourteen-year-old eyes popped out of their sockets.

I mumbled, "I think so," as I quickly lowered my head, pen in hand, and began writing.

However, I certainly didn't write down that the pre-Clear had disrobed and that we were now in a topless auditing session.

I also audited a large, muscular black man who looked like he might have been a professional body builder. His large muscles rippled beneath his sheer tank top. As a small, young teenager, he seemed a bit intimidating to me due to his physical size.

Perhaps not surprisingly, there were very few, if any, people of color involved in Scientology at Celebrity Centre, or in Scientology in general. I think I encountered him and maybe two other black Scientologists. In the 1970s, Scientology seemed to attract mostly white, privileged consumers who could afford their services.

Sitting across from each other in a small particleboard cubicle, I began the auditing session by asking him to hold the cans attached to the e-meter. As I started the prescribed questioning, I watched the e-meter needle move and wrote my notes on blank white paper using a blue pen. Standard operating procedure for auditing sessions.

But during this questioning, I recorded some very interesting, albeit disturbing, information. The man told me he was living in the Celebrity Centre dorms with other Scientologists. Not unusual. However, somehow, in response to one of my questions, he revealed that while "sleeping" near another male Scientologist, a young white male, he awoke to find white liquid on the sheets.

Even at fourteen years old, this sounded a little fishy to me. Granted, I knew nothing, and I mean nothing, about homosexuality or homosexual behavior, aside from what mommy had shared with me about daddy. But I did have enough emotional intelligence and intuition to know that this man was watching me and waiting for my reaction. Well, the e-meter went wacky. The needle starting slamming right and left. A sign that possible lies, or as Scientologists called it, "enturbulating thoughts" were surfacing.

Frazzled by what the man told me, and by the frantic behavior of the e-meter's needle, I turned five different shades of pink and quickly ended the auditing session. But the man didn't seem bothered or upset. He just smiled at me as we both got up and left the cubicle.

Afterward, I carried his pre-Clear folder to the designated area and left it on the pile of folders that waited to be read, commented on, and given directives for the next auditing session. But as I walked home from Celebrity Centre, I thought about what he'd told me. Something seemed not quite right, but I didn't really understand what it was.

Little did I know that the large man who sat across from me in the auditing cubicle at Celebrity Centre was molesting a young boy in the dormitory room they shared. I was too inexperienced and naïve myself to really grasp the descriptions that he provided and the enormity of his deeds. But as a well-trained auditor, I wrote them down in my auditing notes, and turned them in for the Case Supervisor to read and provide insights and directions for our next auditing steps.

Those next steps included grilling me about what had transpired between the man and the young boy. I was asked about the white stains on the sheets and the man's account of how they got there by another supervising Scientologist, whose job was to determine the allegations and to bury them as quickly as possible. After sharing what I knew, which were the details the man had calmly stated during our auditing session, I was told that I'd no longer be this man's auditor. Case closed.

The following week, I learned that the man had left Celebrity Centre. I'm not sure if he went to another Org or if the molestation was ever addressed. No one ever spoke to me again about what I'd heard during our auditing session, or how I might have felt about the incident. I was just assigned a new pre-Clear folder.

When the information was shared with me, it was very matter of fact. The Scientologist who told me probably thought I understood completely what had happened. He also knew I wouldn't question how Scientology handled the incident. Needless to say, it was one of many instances when Scientology covered up and denied any wrongdoing. To my knowledge, no actions were ever taken by the young boy who was being molested or by any Scientologists to save him from this abuse.

⎯⎯⊗⊗⊗⎯⎯

DODGING A BULLET,
CIRCA 1975

One afternoon, two Scientology male Sea Org members, young guys in white shirts and dark pants, came to our apartment. The knock on the door was unexpected, but I decided to see who was there.

After opening the door, I stood in the doorway, surprised and slightly embarrassed that these two Scientologists, guys I knew from Celebrity Centre, had come to look for me at the apartment.

I'd just turned sixteen years old, and I hadn't been going to Celebrity Centre for over six months. Before that though, I'd been a fairly active Scientologist, paying for some training courses. Although, actually, it was my parents who paid. I was also still an auditor with several pre-Clears whom I had auditing sessions with.

In spite of the incident with the Scientologists who lived in the dorms at Celebrity Centre, I loved auditing. My favorite part was writing case notes and turning them into the Case Supervisor, then anxiously waiting to receive positive comments such as, "Pre-Clear is making gains. Well Done!" written in red pen. It felt just like school. I definitely liked the accolades as well as the perceived importance of being an auditor.

But the last time I'd seen the two Scientologists who were at my door was right before mommy and I had an argument. I'd just returned home from a Scientology event where I'd been given the "hard sell" on joining the Sea Org. Even though I wasn't yet eighteen years old, I could still join and sign the billion-year contract without parental permission. Or at least that's what I was told.

I immediately began packing a bag of clothes to take with me. I was ready to go! My teenage mentality couldn't truly fathom the time frame of a billion years. I just wanted to get out of the house and away from mommy, who was hysterical when I told her my plan. She knew what it would mean if I joined the Sea Org. She probably saw my life flashing before her eyes.

Only mommy and I were in my room. I'm not sure if my little brother was in the apartment. Daddy was in the convalescent home, forgotten and abandoned by both his family and Scientology. Once he became too sick to pay for more training and auditing, Scientology seemed to turn its back on him.

When mommy told Scientologists at the local org about the sad progression of daddy's illness, and why he was no longer taking courses or paying for auditing, she wasn't surprised by their reaction. She told me Scientology believed that if your body wasn't working for you anymore, that it was time to "drop" the one you were in and get a new one. That never made sense to me, but I also never questioned this thinking. It wasn't allowed.

Standing in my bedroom, emptying my dresser drawers into the bag, mommy and I screamed at each other for a few minutes.

"Pamela, put that bag down!"

"No!" I screamed back, "I'm leaving!"

We continued to argue. I eventually slammed my bedroom door in her face as she screamed at me, "I'll call the police if you try to leave and join the Sea Org. You're a minor. It's against the law!"

Angrily jamming my underwear, socks, t-shirts, and jeans into a duffel bag, I thought about what she'd just said. Could she stop me? Would the police follow me? I'm not sure if she really would have called the cops, but it got my attention and I reconsidered.

When I finally opened the door to my bedroom and walked out to the living room, I saw mommy seated at the dining room table with a cigarette in her hand and an ashtray full of cigarette butts next to her package of Kools.

I could tell she'd been crying. I watched as she dabbed at her runny nose and red eyes between sniffs. Her tears had disrupted the make-up on her face, leaving tiny streaks across her cheeks.

Neither of us spoke as I continued walking toward the kitchen. I turned my head slightly and glanced at her as I opened the refrigerator. But I wasn't really hungry or thirsty. I turned toward her, keeping my distance in the kitchen. I wondered what she was going to do next. Had she called the police? I also thought about how she might try to keep me away from Scientology.

We both remained silent for a few more minutes as I stood in the kitchen, and mommy puffed on her cigarette. She picked up the empty cigarette package lying on the table and fiddled with the cellophane wrapper. We were both in our respective corners, waiting for one of us to make the next move.

Slowly, she put the tissue down next to the full ashtray and looked up at me. She didn't look angry, just sort of sad and tired.

"Pamela," she started, calling me by my full name, which she never used, unless she was angry with me. Her tone was firm, "I know you can't understand why I won't let you join the Sea Org, but I can't."

"Why not?" I asked, feeling rebellious.

She looked at me with no hint of emotion now, just determination. "Do you think that being in the Sea Org will make you happy?"

Happier than here, I thought.

"Yes," I answered.

She continued questioning me, "What do you think will happen when you join the Sea Org?"

I hadn't considered this question, just that I wouldn't be in our apartment anymore, and that I'd get to wear a uniform like all the Sea Org recruits I'd met at the Orgs.

"I'm not sure." Then I quickly added, "I'll go to Celebrity Centre and have fun." And I confidently stated, "I'll make money."

Mommy's mouth opened wide as she began laughing. Hurt and confused, I scowled at her, but she couldn't contain herself. Her laughter filled the room. I watched as her shoulders shook and her eyes began to water. Finally, her laughter subsided, and she took a drag on what was left of her lit cigarette sitting in the ashtray, amongst the snuffed-out butts and gray ashes.

Looking straight into my eyes, her voice was unflinching as she began her tirade, "Oh, yes, it will be lots of fun. Working day and night, sleeping in a dumpy house with other brainwashed Sea Org recruits. You won't even have your own room. As for making money, that's a joke! Do you know how little they make?"

Incredulous, I couldn't understand why she'd laughed at me, and why she was telling me how bad the Sea Org was. Wasn't she a Scientologist? Didn't she know that Sea Org members were smart and important?

Having heard enough, I walked back to my bedroom and slammed the door. I'm not sure why, but that day, I decided not to leave and join the Sea Org. Maybe it was partly because I'd begun exploring the real world outside the walls of Scientology, spending much of my time with school friends, and other teenagers, especially cute teenage boys who were closer to my own age, including my new boyfriend.

I met him in November of 1975. He belonged to a youth organization, but lived in a different city. I began flirting with him at one of the sponsored events, a bowling tournament. I didn't have a ride home from the event as I'd come with other kids who left early, or at least that was my story. My best friend at the time prodded and encouraged me to go up to him and ask if he could give us a ride home. He seemed amused by our request, but he agreed, and our romance began.

Standing in the hallway, outside our apartment, the two Scientologists didn't enter, and I didn't invite them in. But they did look over me and into our apartment. It was easy to see over my petite five-foot-two-inch frame. What they saw was my boyfriend standing in the living room, tall and athletic at six-feet-five inches. But he didn't deter them from talking to me.

"Hey, Pam, we haven't seen you around for a while," one of the guys said.

The other guy asked, "So what's been going on?"

Well, it was pretty obvious that my boyfriend was what had been going on. For whatever reason, possibly the timing or their lack of courage to say more as they confronted a very tall and slightly intimidating "wog," a Scientology term for a nonScientologist, they didn't try their "hard sell" on me that afternoon.

I sincerely believe that if my boyfriend hadn't been at my apartment with me, perhaps if just mommy or I had opened the door, I may have been strong-armed into joining the Sea Org.

But the guys didn't want a scene. They weren't on their home turf. Out in the real world, they didn't have as much clout or persuasive ability to control the outcome. Scientology bullies lose their superpowers when they leave their insulated bubble.

That was my last formal encounter with Scientologists. In hindsight, I'm thankful for mommy's threats to call the cops when I entertained the idea of signing a billion-year contract, and for my boyfriend's presence that day. My story would be very different had I joined the Sea Org, as so many broken families can attest.

At the end of the summer, after the argument with mommy and the visit from the Scientologists, school resumed and I became more involved in the youth organization that my boyfriend belonged to. I spent my weekends attending events, parties, and fundraisers that supported the organization. Car washes were the best, along with formal dances that required wearing long, fancy dresses.

And, at sixteen, I saw in my boyfriend everything that I wanted. I truly believed that meeting him had given me the promise of a new life, one that might afford me all that my teenage psyche yearned for: a chance to fit in and to live a normal life. Little did I know how difficult and unrealistic my expectations would become.

I never told anyone in the youth club that I was involved in Scientology. Although my boyfriend knew a little about it, due to the visit that day at my apartment, he really didn't ask too many questions, and I didn't talk about it. I was too afraid to let him know about my past. I was certain he would view me differently if he knew my secrets. I felt conflicted and unsure of how to mesh my Scientology life with this new life.

TAKING CARE OF DADDY, LONG BEACH, CALIFORNIA, CIRCA 1977

When I finished high school, daddy was moved to the VA hospital in Long Beach, California, after suffering multiple bladder infections at the convalescent home, and due to his weakening muscles and overall poor health. This would be his final home.

But before that, immediately after daddy was placed in the convalescent home, mommy began seeing Keith, a somewhat older man who lived in our apartment building. As their "romance" blossomed, mommy often stayed very late at night in Keith's downstairs apartment. He also frequently stayed the night at our apartment, which became annoying. The problem with him in our apartment was not so much that he was a drunk, but that he'd get up in the middle of the night looking for the bathroom and stumble loudly into my bedroom.

Mommy would wake up and hear him. Then she'd yell for him to come back to bed. But she usually had to physically get up and steer him back into her room. Of course, I pretended to be asleep during the commotion. I really didn't see the attraction, and I certainly didn't think mommy was exercising good judgment. Keith was also kind of a narcissist who didn't like kids. It was no secret that he wasn't particularly fond of me or my little brother, and the feeling was definitely mutual.

Maybe because she was working, or maybe because of Keith, during the few years that daddy was in the VA hospital, mommy only took me to visit him once. Walking into daddy's room, I saw him lying under a white sheet in his hospital bed. He looked smaller, but he could still carry on a conversation and seemed to be in fairly good spirits.

He even introduced mommy to the nursing staff as his wife. I looked over at mommy and saw her physically shudder and then quickly put on a pretend smile. Little did daddy know that she was in the process of secretly divorcing him so she could marry Keith.

Before we left, I bent down and told daddy, "I love you," as I gave him a hug and a kiss on the forehead.

Daddy smiled, held my hand, and gave me a peck on the cheek. I felt sorry for him, and angry at mommy for being with Keith and for not telling daddy the truth.

"All right, well, I guess it's time to go," mommy said.

She left his room first. I followed, turning to wave to daddy before opening the door and walking out. As mommy and I walked down the hallway of the hospital, I wondered when I would see daddy again. I didn't drive, and getting to Long Beach would mean quite a long bus ride. Mommy and I didn't talk much on the ride home and definitely not about daddy.

. . .

When I was eighteen years old, I moved out of the condo I'd been living in with mommy, Keith, and my brother, who was not so little anymore. Since their relationship had become more serious, mommy had convinced Keith that they needed to find a bigger place for all of us to live. It was in Glendale, a suburb of Los Angeles.

Needless to say, I wasn't happy about our new living arrangements, nor the longer distance to get to work and school. I was now attending Los Angeles City College, and it took about an hour on several different buses to get to the campus.

I'd saved enough money from my part-time job and the Disability checks I received because of daddy to move out, which I did, right after my eighteenth birthday. I found a very small duplex in L.A. that a friend and I rented. It was close to work and school and more importantly, to my boyfriend.

But soon after I moved, I started receiving phone calls. The first time it happened, I called mommy, who I started calling, "mom," after no longer living with her and turning eighteen, which seemed appropriate, now that I was older and on my own.

"Hi, mom," I said. "How are you?"

"I'm good. How are you?"

I didn't answer her question, and I didn't know how to tell her, so I just blurted it out: "The VA hospital just called about dad."

Calmly, she replied, "Oh, what did they say?"

I thought to myself, Doesn't she think it's odd that they called me and not her? But I answered her anyway, thinking she might be worried to learn that he had an infection.

"They told me that dad has a bladder infection, and that I need to authorize the medication for the infection."

Casually, as if I was telling her something insignificant or unimportant, she asked, "Oh, what did you tell them?"

I quickly responded, "I didn't know what to tell them so I called you."

But what I wanted to really say was, you are his wife and I am his daughter and this is not my responsibility, it is yours.

Without missing a beat, she nonchalantly said, "Oh, well you can tell them to authorize it, if you want to."

What? I thought. Why would I authorize it? You are his wife. I don't think it is my responsibility, is it?

Instead, I asked her, "Mom, I'm just wondering why they called me and not you?"

"Oh, because you are the designated family member," she stated as a matter of factual information.

Shocked, I thought, What? Since when? Why didn't she tell me?

Trying my best to stay calm and sound grown-up, I told her, "Mom, I didn't know that."

"Oh, I know. I hadn't told you because I wasn't sure if the hospital would call you this soon," she replied.

Bewildered, I thought, What does she mean by this soon? Have they called before? What else has been wrong with him?

"Mom," I almost whined, "I'm worried that dad is sick. Do we need to go see him?"

"Oh, no," she quickly replied. "He gets bladder infections frequently. It's because of the catheter. You just need to authorize the medicine. He'll be fine."

Trying to comprehend what she was telling me, I felt like I was fumbling over my words. "I didn't know about his bladder infections. How many has he had?"

Before she could answer, I asked, "Mom, why am I the designated family member?"

"Oh," she replied, "because your dad and I are no longer legally married. I filed for a divorce and the paperwork is final now."

I'm not sure why, but I wasn't surprised by her response. I guess I knew that eventually this was going to happen, but I wasn't sure how to react.

"I didn't know that," I said.

"I know. I hadn't told you yet."

Dismissing both mom and her reply, I told her, "OK. I'm going to call the hospital back. Maybe we can talk later this week."

As always, she seemed oblivious to my feelings as she replied, "Okay, honey. I love you. I'll talk to you later. Bye."

Unable to tell her that I loved her, too, I simply replied, "Bye, mom," and hung up quickly.

After hanging up the phone, I burst into tears and cried. What a mess! I had moved out on my own in an attempt to finally get away from her and all her crazy behavior, including her bad choices with men, and she drops this on me. I thought, How did I become the responsible adult in this scenario?

Divorcing daddy seemed cold and calculating, as if she'd planned for me to have to take care of him because she wanted her freedom. It seemed selfish. But why was I surprised?

Wiping my tears, I picked up the phone again and called the VA hospital back to authorize the medicine. This was the first of many calls.

· · ·

Sadly, I only visited daddy one more time in the VA hospital before he died. A few months before his death, a psychologist or maybe a psychiatrist, who was assigned to his case, called mom. She told the doctor that she was legally divorced from my dad and that she needed to speak to his daughter. Mom relayed this information to me somewhat nonchalantly over the phone.

I called the hospital number that she provided and spoke with a woman who asked, "Hello, is this Paul's daughter?"

"Yes," I replied.

Without any warning or pleasantries, she stated, "Your father is very depressed."

"Oh...." Shocked by her declaration about my dad, my voice trailed off. I didn't know how to respond.

The woman waited for me to say more, but when I didn't, she asked, "When was the last time you visited him?"

I was silent. I didn't remember. I knew I hadn't seen him in more than a year, maybe longer.

"I'm not sure. I don't drive and it is hard to get there," I stammered into the phone, feeling guilty for not visiting him.

She immediately responded, "Well, he wants to see you. Can you come and visit him?"

Curious that daddy had told her that he wanted to see me, I replied, "Yes, I think so."

I knew that I'd need to ask my boyfriend to drive me there, because I was pretty sure mom wouldn't. Besides, I really didn't want to go with her. Anyway, daddy had asked to see me, not her. The woman seemed pleased with my response.

"Good," she replied. When can you come?"

I had no idea, so I told her, "I need to check. Probably on the weekend."

"Okay," she told me. I'll put that in the notes." Again, she seemed pleased that she'd accomplished her goal.

Then she added, "He's not doing very well."

Surprised by her final comment, I answered, "Oh, okay. I didn't know that. Thank you," and we both hung up.

• • •

My boyfriend drove me to the Veterans' Hospital in Long Beach on a sunny Sunday afternoon. I'd told him earlier about the conversation with the woman from the hospital. He encouraged me to go and see my dad, especially since they had called.

When I thought about it, it was as if I'd almost tried to forget that daddy was sick and in the hospital, except when they called to tell me that he had a bladder or kidney infection, and asked me to authorize his medication. My wanting to forget made me, I believe, not visit.

The hospital was huge and I had no idea where to find him. We asked for assistance at the entrance and were directed to another building. Once there, we inquired again, and were told the floor and the room number. I walked down a very long white tiled hallway to his room. My boyfriend waited for me by the elevator.

Once I found his room, I opened the closed bluish-colored door. It was heavy. I walked inside and looked for daddy. He was in a bed against the wall. The only other furniture in the room was a metal and vinyl chair and a nightstand next to the bed. I could barely see his head sticking out from under the grayish-white hospital sheet and blanket. He looked so small, like he had shrunk.

His eyes were closed, but he opened them as I walked toward him and said, "Hi, daddy. It's Pam."

Standing next to the side of the bed, I could see how small his body had become, almost skeletal. His shoulder bones protruded from under the thin hospital gown that covered his upper body. His legs, two small bumps that caused the covers to rise slightly just beneath his torso, were also hidden. Walking to the side of the bed, I saw his thin arms and bony fingers lying motionless on the top of the covers, next to his shrunken frame. I was shocked by how different he looked. He was not the daddy I remembered.

He smiled as best he could. As his lips parted and moved, I could see his stained, decaying yellow teeth. His eyes were moist and glossy, but they were still the green that I knew, the same color as my eyes. He started to speak, but trying to open his mouth seemed difficult. Only sounds that didn't resemble words came out. They were really just utterances.

But I pretended that I heard, "I love you," as I answered back, "I love you, too, daddy."

I touched his fingers and his hand. They were cold, icy. I had no idea how close to death he was. I had no concept of dying. At nineteen years old, I was doing my best to navigate college courses, work, life with my roommate, and dating my boyfriend. Daddy, his illness, and Scientology were almost distant memories, no longer part of my life.

Yet being in that room with him, his shriveled body, and the smell of his urine made me feel sorry for him. He'd truly been abandoned by me, his family, and Scientology. Only due to his short stint in the U.S. Navy was he able to even access healthcare at the Veterans' hospital. Otherwise, he would have been truly destitute, and probably dead already.

With my hand on top of his, he tried to move his fingers, to hold onto mine, but his efforts were futile. His smile left his face and his eyes became even moister. He looked sad.

Then he tried to tell me something else. It seemed important for him to get out the words, even though it was difficult for him to move his mouth and utter sounds. Laboriously, he kept making the same sounds as he looked at me intently.

Not knowing what to do, I said, "I know, daddy. It's okay. I love you." As I held his hand and smiled at him, he became quiet. He looked tired.

I stood next to his bed for a minute more in the silence. His gaze was still on me, but he didn't try to say anything else. I let go of his hand and told him that I would see him again soon. He smiled a little, without opening his mouth, and I turned to walk out of the room.

When I got to the heavy door, I turned and looked at him one last time before opening the door and walking out. I felt so sad. He'd become nothing. Important to no one, not even to me, his daughter. He'd been abandoned by his wife years ago, and deserted by his "religion" years before that.

As I approached the elevator, my boyfriend was waiting for me. He asked me how it went, and I started to cry. He held me, and I told him I wanted to go home to my apartment. We didn't talk much on the drive home. I felt tired and angry, resenting mom for divorcing daddy and for leaving me to deal with visiting him and taking the calls from the hospital. But I also thought about how he'd been trying to tell me something important.

After a while, my boyfriend asked me, "Were you able to talk to your dad?"

"Yes," I replied, "a little."

I didn't feel like explaining or describing how bad daddy looked, or how difficult it had been for him to talk.

"What did you say?" he asked.

"I told him that I loved him," I shared.

"That's good," he replied.

My boyfriend truly believed that love was the answer. We both did. As we turned down the street to my apartment, I told him that it was probably best if he didn't come in, and that I wanted to be alone. He looked a bit dejected, but said that he understood. He told me to call him later. I told him I would.

Luckily, my roommate and her boyfriend were not in the apartment. I hoped they'd be gone for a while. I went into my bedroom, climbed under my flowered comforter, and sobbed uncontrollably into my pillow. Stopping to catch my breath between sobs, I yelled loudly, as if my mother could hear me, "Why did you put him in the hospital? Just because he was sick?"

Finally, my rant and my sobs subsided. Lying on my back, under the covers, staring at the ceiling, I told myself, daddy was trying to tell me something important. What was it? You heard him. He just couldn't make the sounds come out right. He heard you tell him it was okay. He heard you say that you loved him.

I got up and went into the small front room of the apartment where the phone sat on a table next to our ugly brown couch. My roommate and I were renting a small, two-bedroom, one-bath apartment in a brown stucco duplex in the middle of Los Angeles, the best we could afford with our minimum wage salaries. I picked up the black receiver from the phone and pushed the buttons to dial my boyfriend's number.

"Hi," I said quietly, cradling the receiver between my chin and my right hand.

"Hi," he replied. He sounded sad. "How are you doing?" he asked.

"I'm okay," I replied meekly, even though I didn't feel okay. I felt depleted and angry.

"Can I see you this week?" he asked, somewhat tentatively.

"Maybe...I think so," I responded cautiously.

I felt fragile and scared, like a little girl who was pretending to be all grown-up. I began crying. Softly, my tears trickled down my cheeks, fell off my chin, and landed on the black receiver. I watched in silence as the drops of water that fell from my eyes dripped down my face. I didn't want him to know that I was crying.

Hearing only silence on the other end, he questioned me.

"Pam, are you still there?" I took a deep breath and answered, "Yeah, I'm still here. I better go now. I hear my roommate at the door," I lied.

"Oh, okay. I'll call you later," he replied. "I love you," he added.

"I love you too," I whispered and hung up the phone.

Walking back to my bedroom, I was consumed by waves of sadness. Regret and rage crashed over me. I climbed back into my bed, clutched my pillow, and covered my head with my comforter.

Between muffled screams and tears, I heard myself say, "I hate you! I hate you!" I wasn't sure who, or what, I hated in that moment. Was it my mom or the realization that daddy was dying?

• • •

Daddy died during the Memorial Day weekend, six years after being diagnosed with MS. After his death, he was cremated. We arranged a burial with the Nautilus Society, which provided a boat and crew to take mom, her new husband, Keith, my brother, me, and my boyfriend, out to sea from the Long Beach Harbor.

Once we were out at sea, just past the harbor rocks, my brother read a brief passage from a Scientology book. Then the two of us opened the plastic bag that held daddy's ashes and dumped them into the sea. His brief time on Earth, just forty-nine years, seemed incomprehensible to me.

His two living sisters didn't join us on the boat. Although one of his sisters lived in California, I'm not sure if she was notified of his death. My grandmother, daddy's mother, had passed away prior to his death. No one from Lockheed where he worked when we first arrived in Los Angeles was informed of his death. He'd lost contact with them after he stopped working. To my knowledge, no Scientologists were told of his death either.

As I was daddy's legal next of kin, due to mom divorcing him, I handled all the arrangements. At nineteen years old, I really couldn't fathom the ramifications of his death, both financially and emotionally.

I don't believe he had any life insurance. But for many years after his death, my brother and I continued to receive Disability checks, due to daddy's status as a disabled veteran. As a college student, the money helped cover the cost of my classes and housing.

In the decades that followed, I chose to mourn his short life by memorializing his physical struggle with Multiple Sclerosis while blocking out my childhood memories of him. Scientology also became a buried part of my life, along with my sexual abuse. Yet his final "words" that day at the VA hospital continued to haunt me. Was he asking for forgiveness? Sadly, I'll never know.

EPILOGUE

Nineteen years later, and seven months after the birth of my fourth daughter, my mom suffered a traumatic brain aneurism and died three days later, after I authorized her to be taken off life support. She was sixty-one years old, just a month shy of turning sixty-two. I was thirty-eight years old.

She was at work and had gone to the break room in the afternoon after lunch. Her office mate, the secretary who worked with her, told me that mom had been complaining of a headache all day. Slumped over the table, they thought she was asleep. But when they tried to wake her, she was disoriented and unable to stand up.

They immediately called the paramedics. The ambulance report stated that the left side of her body was in a state of paralysis. She was resuscitated in the back of the ambulance as they drove her to the hospital. The CT scan that was taken clearly showed that blood had filled both sides of her brain.

I received a call from the hospital shortly after she was admitted. Driving there with my husband, which took about an hour, I dreaded seeing her. I wasn't sure what to expect. The doctor shared her CT scan images, as well as her prognosis with me in an honest and very matter-of-fact manner. He was not hopeful.

I sat in the ICU hospital room and stared at mom. She was basically being kept alive by a ventilator and medication to help alleviate some of the swelling in her brain. Except for the ventilator pushing air in and out of her lungs, she made no movements. The only sounds in the room came from the machines that were keeping her alive and her weak coughs. A smoker her entire life, she was still suffering the effects in her lungs even after her brain was filled with blood.

I left her room and called my brother. If the decision to take mom off life support had to be made, I didn't want to make it alone. Truthfully, though, my brother, my mom, and I really hadn't been a family for a very long time.

He now lived in the Midwest, where he'd moved with his wife and two sons. They'd left L.A. years earlier, after my brother received a lucrative and appealing job offer from an art and media company, moving to a quieter, more-rural lifestyle where they could afford a home and raise their family. Mom even traveled to see them a few times to visit and spend time with her grandsons.

When my brother arrived at the hospital, after flying to Los Angeles alone, he saw mom hooked up to a ventilator and other machines, lying in the ICU bed. Looking at her for a few moments, he seemed convinced that mom was gone. I wasn't so sure. But he didn't seem to have as much trouble letting go of her.

That night, while visiting mom in the ICU, I spoke with the nurse who was attending her. I thanked her for taking care of mom, and asked her how she managed to do her job each day when patients, like my mom, were dying.

She told me, "I know that I'm good at what I do. Making people comfortable at the end of their lives is important."

She must have sensed that I was struggling with the decision to either keep mom on the ventilator or to take her off, thus letting her die.

Kindly, while fixing the blankets to cover up mom's thin shoulders, which slightly protruded underneath a blue hospital gown, she asked, "Would it help if you could read the report from the ambulance?"

Surprised by her question, I replied, "I'm not sure. I guess so."

She went to mom's chart and opened a folder. After turning a few pages of paper, she found the report.

"Here," she said, "Maybe this will help."

Reading the factual explanation of what had transpired during mom's final minutes was difficult. I wondered if she knew that she'd suffered a debilitating and deadly stroke or if she was just confused until she lost consciousness in the back of the ambulance. The report noted that she tried to look at her watch on her left wrist, but she couldn't move her arm due to the paralysis.

Learning that she was resuscitated in the back of the ambulance provided me with more information. She had stopped breathing, but was brought back to life. Her body had begun to shut down, and her heart would have soon stopped. She'd been given time. Time to let her family and friends visit her, although it was only my brother, my husband, and me who were present at the hospital. Maybe the time was for us.

On the final day, before she died, I called my mom's older brother, Jesse, and told him about his sister.

I could hear the sadness in his voice on the other end of the phone as he said, "Glory wouldn't want to be like this. It's time for her to go."

As hard as it was to hear those words, I felt as though he knew her best. Better than any of her husbands, friends, or Scientologists, and certainly better than her children. I thanked him and told him I was going to authorize turning off her life support. He told me to take care and that he knew it was hard. I wasn't close to my uncle, and I hadn't seen him or my cousins in decades, but his words gave me guidance and some courage.

Before I authorized mom's death, I sat in her hospital room and stared at her, looking at her long, thin legs and arms underneath the hospital gown and covers. Her feet were bare, and they were sticking out from underneath the bottom of the bedsheet. At the end of her slender feet and ankles, her toes were painted a pretty pink.

She looked peaceful, as if she was sleeping. I could hear the steady sound of the machine that was pumping her stomach, due to the strong medications she was being given, along with the sound of the ventilator. Occasionally, she would cough, breaking the rhythm of these machines, reminding me that she was still alive, but not present.

I felt sad for her. She was not yet retired. Her life had been cut short and she'd never be able to enjoy it again. I also thought about how she'd finally escaped from Scientology, as well as from her addictive, abusive second husband to live a life she chose. It seemed as if she'd finally found a job she liked, some friends who she enjoyed, and a hobby she was passionate about, playing bridge.

Watching her chest rise and fall as the ventilator allowed her to breathe, I pondered the many bad decisions she'd made in her life and wondered why this had to happen now. Why couldn't she have lived longer, long enough for the two of us to build a relationship, one that would have included love, not hate?

I'd spoken to her on the phone a few weeks before she suffered the aneurism. It was late January, after the holidays, and we were planning to get together for Valentine's Day. We'd made a lunch date.

At the end of the conversation, I said, "I love you."

She told me, "I love you, too. I'm looking forward to seeing you soon."

That was it.

We'd both tried hard to heal our wounds. Time had helped. Raising my daughters and building my own family gave me perspective. Being a mother is hard work even without the constant influence of a crazy cult.

I mourned mom's death for years. As dysfunctional as our relationship had been throughout my childhood, I mourned what could have been. We'd started down the path to healing, but only a few small steps had been taken. There was a whole road ahead of us that now could no longer be accessed. She was once again unreachable. The finality of her death closed the door on that chapter of my life. I was no longer abandoned, just parentless, orphaned.

But prior to her untimely death, mom had made one final Scientology connection with a man named Don Breeding. He'd been involved in Scientology since the 1950s, like my parents. A year or two before she died, she started seeing him, going out on lunch and dinner dates. She casually shared this information with me at one of my daughters' birthday parties.

As we cleaned up after the party, walking around the backyard, picking up half-drunk cups of juice and half-eaten plates of birthday cake, she nonchalantly mentioned, "I went out to lunch with Don Breeding. Do you remember him?"

Puzzled, I replied, "No, I don't. Who is he?"

Lighting a cigarette, holding the slender white object between her fingers, she told me, "He's a Scientologist. I think you might have seen him at one of the Orgs or maybe on the ship."

Stunned, then angry, I thought, What the hell?! Why is she dating a Scientologist? Is she crazy?

Mustering up all my patience and courage, I coolly yet clearly replied, "Mom, that period of my life was a nightmare. I just want to forget about it."

She looked at me, a little taken aback. Taking a long drag on her now-lit cigarette, she calmly said, "Oh, okay. I didn't know that."

Door closed, conversation over. That was the only time, really, that we ever spoke of Scientology and how I felt about it.

Days after mom's death, while going through her personal

belongings, like her checkbook, and her address book, I found Don's phone number. I'm not sure why, but I decided to call him. Maybe I thought he could provide some insights into her connection with Scientology again, after all those years. He answered the phone, and after briefly introducing myself as Gloria's daughter, I blurted out that she'd died.

He was genuinely surprised, and possibly saddened, as he told me that he'd seen her a few times in the last year, but shared that he hadn't heard from her in a while. Offering an explanation, he told me that he'd been "seeing" pictures of empty office cubicles coming from where mom worked. "That explains why I haven't heard from her. She was showing me what was going on. She was letting me know that she was no longer there."

As a Scientologist, he truly believed that these "images" were evidence of their "telepathic" communication.

As Don continued talking, I learned that he and my parents met in Washington, D.C. in 1957 at the first Church of Scientology. They were Hubbard Association of Scientologists associates and fellow Scientologists. In 1958, Don, an engineer by trade, helped L. Ron Hubbard, and Scientology, by reimagining the e-meter. He designed and built the new Hubbard Electrometer, which replaced the original Mathison e-meter, designed by Volney Mathison.

In the early 1950s, at the onset of Dianetics auditing in Wichita, Kansas, Hubbard had been paying Mathison royalties for the use of the original e-meter, along with his instruction manuals on how to audit people with the device. But Mathison was unwilling to sell Hubbard his patent. By eliminating the e-meter and ordering all auditors to go back to using Dianetics auditing procedures without it, Hubbard could save money. In the *Professional Auditors Bulletin Number* (PAB) 52 of 13 May 1955, Hubbard wrote:

> *"And here come E-Meters back into the picture. The HAS is, at this moment, building a new and better E-Meter than has ever been built before, under the trademarked name of Physio-galvanometer, or O-Meter. It has very little in common with the old type E-Meter. Nevertheless, an old type E-Meter can be utilized."*

I wondered if Don was ever paid royalties or any sizable monetary amount for his design. I didn't ask, but thought, Most likely not. L. Ron Hubbard had convinced the HAS members of his mantra, "the greatest good for the greatest number of dynamics," meaning that which is good for the group (Scientology) is more important and takes precedence over that which is good for the individual. Unless, of course, it was good for Hubbard, which took precedence over everything that occurred in Scientology, especially when it came to money.

After chatting with Don a few minutes more, I also learned that he'd been publishing an old-timers' newsletter for Scientologists. It contained stories about older Scientologists, some who'd been involved in Scientology, like my parents, for decades.

I told him that my mom, Gloria, had written some poems. I'd found her writing, while cleaning out her apartment. I mentioned one poem in particular that was about thetans. I wondered if he might possibly want to publish it in his newsletter. He asked me to send it to him.

After hanging up the phone, I didn't think much more about my conversation with Don. But I did send him a copy of mom's poem. It seemed like an appropriate way to possibly honor her involvement in Scientology in a positive way.

Several weeks later, a copy of his newsletter arrived at my house by mail. This is an excerpt from his newsletter, explaining our conversation and his relationship with my mom:

The next day on Thursday I received a telephone call from a girl who identified herself as Pam Williams. "You probably don't remember me," she said, and I allowed that I did not. She went on to say that she had been going through her mother's things… correspondence and all to discover the names of various friends in order to inform them that her mother, Gloria Nickel, had died of a cerebral aneurism the month before on February 5th.

Well, the shock was great…now I knew why Gloria had not answered my several messages over the last many weeks. I also knew why these images I had been getting in the last weeks whenever I drove by her office where she had worked…these images of glass, partitions, desks, and hallways…why these kept cropping up. For I personally had never been in her office and I suddenly perceived that she had been trying to communicate with me as a thetan. I had almost been tempted to stop in and see her, and if I had, of course, would've been told that she was gone.

So, now I'd like to tell you a little about her. She was born March 27, 1934, in Kansas, City, Kansas the daughter of Jessie and Ruby Gorman. She attended Kansas City University for about two years, from what her daughter Pam tells me, and was quite artistically talented.

When I met her in 1957, she was married to Paul Nickel, and they were staff members at the Founding Church of Scientology in Washington, D.C., Paul was by avocation a body builder, and Gloria was a pretty redhead…and who is ever going to forget a good-looking redhead, you know.

Anyhow, after I left staff in Washington, I lost track of them, hearing only that they had moved to New Orleans. I did bump into Gloria with her children in tow once at Saint Hill in England, when she was there doing the Clearing Course. After that I heard nothing and then, about two and a half years ago, I discovered that she was living alone in Glendale as, somewhat ironically, Paul had died of Multiple Sclerosis. Her children had grown up and were married and she had grandchildren (six in all now).

I renewed an old acquaintance and took her to visit the LRH Life Exhibition where she bought several books and then we joined the Huntington Library in a joint membership in order to explore the art exhibits there.

Gloria was also a Life Master at bridge, head of her local bridge club, and well-known nationally in tournaments. And she was certainly a world traveler, often using her vacations to tour various countries and places from which she would send many postcards to her friends, me among them.

The evidence is she in private life was a prolific poet, something which was not revealed to me until her daughter Pam kindly read to me the poem that she also had read at her mother's funeral.

"A Thetan's Harvest"
The seeds of hopes and dreams are not sown upon the soil.
For we do not grow them in the earth with sun and rain and toil.
But clasp them deep within our breast and water them with tears.
We nurture them with love and shelter them from fears.
We hoe away the weeds of doubt, distrust, and pain.
And if they fail to sprout, we plant the seeds again.
We give to them the light that shines down from our goal.
And keep them ever-growing there in the garden of our soul.
For they give to us the purpose of our efforts and our life.
Thus, we labor through the years unbent by struggle or by strife.
Drawing strength upon the knowledge that someday we shall see
Flowers from those seeds because their blooms will be
Hopes and dreams that have become reality.

– Gloria Gorman Nickel

Mom's funeral was attended by a small number of acquaintances, a handful of my friends, my husband's family members, our four daughters, my brother, and me. Jesse, her one living brother, and his wife did not come to California. Both of mom's parents had died years earlier.

Most of those attending the service either worked with mom or knew her from playing bridge. No Scientologists were present. She was cremated and interred at Forest Lawn Mortuary in Los Angeles. I struggled with which name to place on her plaque, and settled on her full name, Gloria Dean Gorman Nickel, as she'd divorced her second husband many years prior to her death.

. . .

Twenty years after my mom's death, I experienced my first clear memory of my sexual abuse. My husband and I had been arguing. As he turned to talk to me, I glanced down at the silver wedding band he wore on his left hand. An image of the pink ruffle that covered the top of my childhood canopy bed flashed before my eyes. I froze. Why was I thinking of my childhood bedroom in the middle of a fight with my husband? The memory didn't go away, but it also didn't change. Just the flutter of the canopy.

Ongoing marital issues propelled me to seek out counseling. I mentioned the fight and the image to my counselor who looked at me and asked, "Do you have any history of sexual abuse?"

Taken aback, I stammered, "Not that I remember."

Like a mirror that has been shattered, slivers of memories started to seep into my consciousness, at surprisingly inopportune moments, like during sex. I learned, that similar to many sexual abuse survivors, I had experienced episodes of disassociation and denial throughout my life. The counselor recommended some specific reading, a book entitled *The Courage to Heal. A Guide for Women Survivors of Child Sexual Abuse* by Ellen Bass and Laura Davis. However, she told me to read it in very small increments.

"Just a little at a time," she cautioned.

After opening the book and reading one survivor's account of the sexual abuse she suffered at the hands of her father, I immediately panicked, put the book away, and decided I would never open it again. I wasn't ready.

Several years later, my husband and I relocated to a small California mountain community. He'd just retired, and I was semiretired. Away from our daughters and close friends, I had many hours to walk in the forest, commune with nature, and to think.

Sitting on my deck, overlooking pine trees, a flood of memories began to fill my head. Childhood stories that I've written about, including the memories of sexual abuse that I experienced as a young child. The more I remembered, the more I wrote.

But instead of seeking out counseling or other forms of assistance, I chose to sift through my memories and my feelings alone, allowing them to wash over me. I tried not to fight the pictures in my head, but instead to capture them on paper as best I could.

During those years, I kept my writing a secret, not even telling my husband. Although he knew some of my Scientology history, I hadn't shared much of it with him, nor with anyone. And my memories of sexual abuse were too fresh, raw, and frightening. I definitely couldn't share them with my family, or even my friends.

One day, after taking a walk in the forest, I'm not sure why, but I chose to open the book that the counselor had recommended years before. I began to slowly read. Just a few pages at a time, in particular the sections about disassociation and healing. I could relate. I identified with being a victim, but I also began to see myself as a survivor. A survivor of both sexual abuse and a survivor of a childhood spent in the cult of Scientology.

The more I learned and remembered about my past, through my own excavation, the more I began to question. Did Scientology enable my dad to sexually abuse me? Or was the environment of Scientology conducive to keeping secrets? As a Scientologist, I knew he couldn't speak his truth, of being both bisexual and a sexual predator, as neither would have been accepted nor condoned. My mom also couldn't speak her truth, as much as she tried.

I also began to wonder if my parents' pathologies were in fact exacerbated by their Scientology beliefs. As Scientologists, when they both confronted their true illnesses, they were met with resistance. Scientology falsely claims that illness and sickness are "pulled in."

In my parents' cases, their illnesses, both physical and mental, were dismissed and perceived as merely manifestations of their thoughts and actions, both overt and covert, that were causing them to become ill, making them believe that it was their own fault.

Throughout my healing journey, I have come to realize that most of what I experienced as a child was not of my own doing. But what did choose, which was perhaps harmful to myself and others, I must forgive in order to heal and move forward.

As a survivor, I have certainly learned that healing takes time. A counselor once told me that the healing process is often as long as, or sometimes longer, than the years of abuse or victimization that the survivor suffered from. No wonder it has taken me so long!

In writing my story, I've been able to clearly see how Scientology and its multilayered practices of intimidation, grooming, and secretiveness are akin to those of sexual predators. As Scientologists, my parents were indoctrinated into a secretive cult. One that established the practice of keeping secrets that were promulgated, and at the same time, fiercely protected by its leader. The secretive nature of Scientology benefited my father while condemning my mother.

My parents also learned well how to hide their lives as Scientologists and how to be accepted into mainstream society. As a child, I lived in both worlds and learned how to navigate between and within the secrets. Today, I am learning to embrace the child who survived.

Clearly, the lies we tell ourselves can be considered true if we believe them. For many years, most of my lifetime, I believed that I was inherently bad, and that I had no control over these feelings. This lie became my truth. But today, in choosing truth over lies, and healing over pain, I've found a way forward, and my own "Road to Total Freedom."

PHOTOGRAPHS

PAM WITH MOMMY & DADDY – COLORADO – CIRCA 1961

PAM – CIRCA 1961

PAM – CIRCA 1962

PAM & DADDY – CIRCA 1960

PAM & LITTLE BROTHER
– CIRCA 1964

COLORADO HOUSE – CIRCA 1962

289

MOMMY & PAM – CIRCA 1962

PAM & DADDY – CIRCA 1961

PAM & DADDY – CIRCA 1960

Little Brother, Mommy & Pam – Passport Photo – Circa 1966

Colorado House in Snow
– Circa 1963

Mommy & Pam – Circa 1962

PAM, LITTLE BROTHER & MOMMY –
JACKSON SQUARE, NEW ORLEANS,LOUISIANA
– CIRCA 1965

PAM & LITTLE BROTHER – SLIDELL, LOUISIANA – CIRCA 1965

PAM – CIRCA 1971

SLIDELL, LOUISIANA, HOUSE – CIRCA 1964 – 1967

MOMMY – CIRCA 1970

LAFAYETTE PARK PLACE – LOS ANGELES, CALIFORNIA – CIRCA 1971

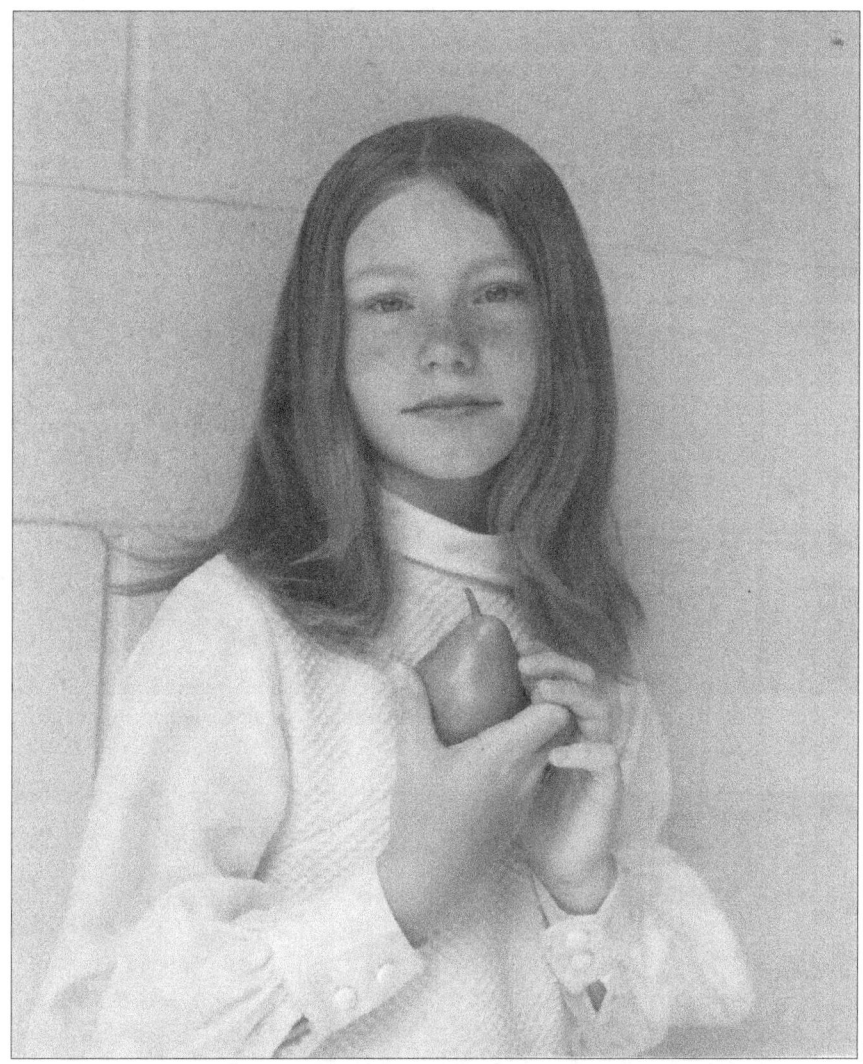

PAM – PHOTO SHOOT – CIRCA 1969

CELEBRITY CENTRE – LOS ANGELES – CIRCA 1970

AMERICAN SAINT HILL ORGANIZATION (ASHO) – LOS ANGELES – CIRCA 1973

Saint Hill Manor – East Grinstead, West Sussex, England – Circa 1967

Harewood Hotel – Tunbridge Wells, Kent, England – Circa 1965

THE *ROYAL SCOTMAN* – CIRCA 1967

ACKNOWLEDGMENTS

It has taken me a lifetime to finally tell my story. Along the way, there have been so many people who have helped to shape and form my beliefs and ideas about the world, about life, and most importantly about love.

First, and foremost, I want to thank my husband, Gill, and my beautiful daughters, Sarah, Cathy, Liz, and Emily for their love, support, and encouragement as I began to share my story with them. I'd also like to thank my little brother for his willingness to allow me to share and speak our family truths.

To my dear friends of over fifty years, Eva and Jeanine, thank you for your consistent and unconditional love, your acceptance, and your support as I shared my secrets and hidden identity as both a Scientology survivor and a survivor of sexual abuse.

So many other friends and family members have also embraced me and my journey, without judgment, allowing me to truly heal by giving me both the time and the space to share my story. Their encouragement has kept me focused on the present and my purpose for writing my book, to help others.

From the beginning, I knew that I would stand on the shoulders of the many ex-Scientologists who have written and shared their stories. I am grateful for their courage, their perseverance, and their factual accounts of their personal experiences in Scientology.

While researching Scientology's history, especially the years that coincided with my story, I relied on many books and resources. Special thanks to Russell Miller, for his book, *Bare-Faced Messiah: The True Story of L. Ron Hubbard*, and Jon Atack for his book, *A Piece of Blue Sky*. Both of these seminal works helped me better understand the history of Scientology and its insidious actions and tactics.

I am especially grateful to Janis Gillham Grady for writing and sharing her story, *The Commodore's Messenger: A Child Adrift in the Scientology Sea Organization*. She has become not only a fellow ex-Scientology traveler to me, but also a friend and resource. Janis's generous support and guidance, along with her ability to still have a sense of humor after all she has survived, helped me stay the course with telling my story.

Many other memoirs, written by fellow ex-Scientologists, including *The Expert Witness: My Life at the Top of Scientology* by Jesse Prince, *The Bad Cadet: Growing Up in the Church of Scientology's Sea Organization* by Katherine Spallino, and *A Billion Years: My Escape From a Life in the Highest Ranks of Scientology* by Mike Rinder provided me with perspective and context in terms of the many eras that have existed in Scientology's history.

Through the writing of my book, I have learned that the ex-Scientology community is a group of highly-gifted and talented individuals who continue to work tirelessly to educate and support those who have chosen to speak out after leaving the cult of

Scientology. Thank you to those of you who have publicly, privately, and generously helped me with telling my story.

Lastly, I am thankful to my editors, Gay Walley and Kuwana Haulsey who guided and helped me with the writing and rewriting of my manuscript. Their expertise and patience were crucial as I chose the best format for memorializing my experiences. Thank you for believing in me as a writer.

Special thanks also to Lara Bessette, my proofreader, for her laser-focused attention to detail. And finally, to Mermaid Cafe for envisioning my book as not just a story, but as an artistic endeavor through the addition of carefully designed chapter images. I am eternally grateful for your help and support.

RESOURCES

This is a brief list of books and websites to support readers on their healing journey.

Sexual Abuse

Books

The Courage to Heal:
A Guide for Women Survivors of Child Sexual Abuse
by Ellen Bass & Laura Davis

The Body Keeps the Score:
Brain, Mind, and Body in the Healing of Trauma
by Bessel van der Kolk

Websites

Rape, Abuse & Incest National Network (RAINN)
& Sexual Assault Hotline:
800.656.HOPE
Anti-sexual violence organization offering prevention,
response, and justice help: **www.rainn.org**

National Center on Domestic Violence,
Trauma, and Mental Health
Promotes survivor-defined healing by transforming the systems
that impact survivors of domestic and sexual violence
and their families: **www.ncdvthmh.org**

Scientology

Books

Bare-Faced Messiah:
The True Story of L. Ron Hubbard
by Russell Miller

Commodore's Messenger:
A Child Adrift in the Scientology Sea
by Janis Gillham Grady

The Bad Cadet:
Growing Up in the Church of Scientology's Sea Organization
by Katherine Spallino

A Billion Years: My Escape from a Life
*in the Highest Rank*s of *Scientology*
by Mike Rinder

Websites

Help for those who want to leave Scientology and the Sea Org:
www.theaftermathfoundation.org

Children of Scientology

Information, support, and resources for Scientology survivors:
www.childrenofscientology.com

A portion of the proceeds
from the sale of this book will be donated
to the Michael J. Rinder Aftermath Foundation,
a nonprofit organization that provides resources,
support, and advocacy to those who leave
Scientology and the Sea Org.

www.ingramcontent.com/pod-product-compliance
Lightning Source LLC
Chambersburg PA
CBHW061557120626
46550CB00004B/1525